Be seen – Be heard – Be remembered

BUILD YOUR A GAME™

Awareness   Affluence
Alliances   Advocate
Authenticity

Carole Sacino

Build Your A-Game, Published March, 2014

Cover Design: Dianne Rux-Leonetti
Interior Design & Layout: Dianne Rux-Leonetti
Editorial & Proofreading: Eden Rivers Editorial Services and Karen Grennan
Photo Credits: David Fox

 SDP Publishing

Published by SDP Publishing, an imprint of SDP Publishing Solutions, LLC.

For more information about this book contact Lisa Akoury-Ross by email at lross@SDPPublishing.com.

All rights reserved. No part of the material protected by this copyright notice may be reproduced or utilized in any form or by any means, electronic or mechanical, including photocopying, recording, or by any information storage and retrieval system, without written permission from the copyright owner.

To obtain permission(s) to use material from this work, please submit a written request to:

SDP Publishing
Permissions Department
36 Captain's Way, East Bridgewater, MA 02333
or email your request to info@SDPPublishing.com

ISBN-13 (print): 978-0-9911597-2-7
ISBN-13 (ebook): 978-0-9911597-3-4
Library of Congress Control Number: 2014931176

Copyright © 2014, Carole Sacino

Printed in the United States of America

Lucinda—

Dedicated to my amazing daughter, Jamie Marie, who is my teacher, student, and inspiration; to my family who loves me for me; and to my parents Maureen and Ray Mercer—I lost both of you way too soon.

Bringing your A Game is for YOU - and your world will change too.

Best

Carole Sacino

Acknowledgments

There are so many people that have influenced and helped me shape my personal and professional life along this journey. It is not possible to name each of you individually, but I would like to thank all of you and present this book in memory of the moments that mattered!

I could not have stayed the course with writing this book without the support, guidance, and "push" I needed to step forward and own my voice throughout these pages.

A very special thanks to my friend and life partner, Jack Lane, for the endless conversations we had over the past few years that continued to validate, encourage, and move me forward in this effort.

And in no particular order, I would like to thank my great friends and resources that have been there for me without judgment, and offered a tremendous amount of encouragement and support throughout the humbling process of writing this book.

With gratitude to Regina Twiss, Nancy Philpott, Lanette Parker, Linda Pogue, Julie Lynch, Peggy McKleroy, Ellen Romanow, Todd Mitchell, Debi Dami, Dianne Thompson, Brad Glass, Deb Busser, Alison Simons, Angela Reich, and Kelly Mount.

A special thanks to Dr. Susan Adams, Betsy Myers, Toni Wolfman, Laura Pollard, Leslie Grossman, Rebecca Schambaugh, Lisa Gates, Victoria Pynchon, Joanna Barsh, Dr. Lois Frankel, Tama Kieves, and Janet Powers for your inspiration and convictions that align with this book.

This project would not have been possible without this dedicated team to keep me on track and on time every step of the way with firmness and a sense of humor too—thank you to Lisa Akoury-Ross, Lisa Schleipfer, Dianne Rux-Leonetti, and Karen Grennan.

Table of Contents

Introduction	7
Chapter One: Building Your A-Game	14
Chapter Two: Awareness	22
The Brain in Mind	22
Energy	32
Personal Needs	48
Values	53
Principles	59
Chapter Three: Authenticity	64
An "Aha" Moment	64
CLARITY	65
Self-Discovery	74
Authenticity and Influence	88
Communication	89
Beyond Networking	101
Build Your Entourage	109
The Difference Between a Mentor and a Sponsor and Why it Matters	118
The Art of Negotiation!	124
Resilience—Building Your Bounce Back!	137
Chapter Four: Alliances/Common-Unity	149
Community	149
Self-Help For Everything!	152
Communities Come In All Flavors	158

Chapter Five: Affluence — 165
Economy — 165
Savvy Women Lead With Their Voices! — 170
The SHE Change (Sea-Change) — 175

Chapter Six: Advocate — 178
Legacy — 178
Pay It Forward — 186

Conclusion — 188
A-Game Terminology — 193
For Research and Further Reading — 201
References — 204

Introduction

Where you're wounded … you're gifted.

I heard this quote the other day while listening to Tama Kieves, author and speaker of *Inspired and Unstoppable*, and one my favorite people that helps the human spirit expand.

It struck a chord and it has played on the main stage of my life as far back as I remember—back to the age of seven. I experienced a huge turning point in my life that I had no idea about at the time, and over the years, had no idea just what gifts had been granted to me.

I am an "Irish twin," one of five children born in six years to very young parents living in the great city of Boston. As you can imagine, the house always was hectic; it was a challenge to get one-on-one time with either parent, especially my mom, and we all required attention at some level.

One day, when I was seven, my grandparents showed up along with other family members to huddle in the kitchen. I knew something definitely was going on. No kids allowed; even though each one of us did try and go in to ask for a drink of water or something to eat.

My parents just had learned that one of their children—"me"— required open-heart surgery if I was to have a good quality of life versus having a life of limitations. The surgery was relatively new and the odds of survival not yet established. Can you imagine having to make this kind of decision for one of your children at any age, but for a seven-year-old?

It was April, 1960, on a cold day in Boston when I had a "special girls day out" with my mom. Just the two of us! I remember exactly what I was wearing that day. I had on a green, plaid, double-breasted coat with a velvet collar; white tights; black Mary

Jane shoes; and a white fur muff to keep my hands warm. I was so excited to have her to myself for the whole day. We went into Boston to do some shopping, have lunch, and then meet up with my two aunts for a show at a local theater that evening. Through all the excitement there was also fear—fear that I would not get to experience this again.

The following week, I went into Boston Children's Hospital for the open-heart surgery. It was a busy place, and I had lots of tests and examinations until it was time for the procedure. My mom and grandfather were with me, holding my hand as they rolled the gurney down a long, bright hall and through the doors into a room filled with masks and machines.

What seemed to be days later I woke up, and I was so delighted to see my grandfather still holding my hand ... I was not sure he ever left my side. He asked me what I would like to drink. I opened my mouth to say, "A strawberry milkshake," and nothing came out! I had NO voice. I could see panic in my mom's face, and the doctor came in, checked me out, and said not to worry, that it was temporary and my voice would return shortly.

Days led into weeks, and continued into months and still ... no voice. I was able to have a soft, raspy, barely-audible voice by the time I was able to go back to school. Between my siblings and the kids in school, the teasing and making fun of me put me into a very sad place. Today they would have called it depression.

And then something made me feel strong and determined to not put up with it anymore.

Knowing that I had a voice—even if you could not hear it—was not going to define me, I was going to define it. It created a very determined streak in me, and the need to prove myself no matter what. That said, this did get in my way more times than not. I found my boldness and determination did create challenges and obstacles throughout my life, along with opportunities and success. Every experience gave me an opportunity to choose moving forward or staying stuck—creating those turning-point moments!

INTRODUCTION

After several months, I did go to speech therapy and learned new ways to use my limited voice in a more effective way. I continued to have a soft, raspy, non-projectable voice that was manageable providing I had no real emotion. If I was scared, the voice would go silent; if I was mad, the voice would go silent; and if I needed to get someone's attention … that was near impossible without a measured approach.

What I learned was that it was not the volume of your voice that mattered; it was what you said and how you said it! Throughout this book I will reflect and share stories, scenarios, obstacles, and opportunities that will help you to **be seen, be heard, and be remembered**.

I was not a great student in school, and was far more fascinated with what was happening in the world with real people, their situations, and their stories. I had a keen observation of human behavior. After all, my voice limitation created the opportunity to be an active listener; I always was present and in the moment in order to seize the chance to be part of the conversation. Believe me, I had plenty to say, yet I found it difficult, and had to learn new strategies to insert myself when the time was right, to be concise and clear and quick with my message. Not only did I have a soft voice, I had a limited capacity to sustain a long-winded conversation. This turned out to be one of the major gifts I received, and was especially useful in my sales career. We will go into this more inside the book.

Another major turning point in my life, and I am sure for most everyone, was September 11, 2001. This had such a profound effect on me, and had me begging the questions: *What is next? Where am I heading? Am I doing what I love? Life can be over in an instant, am I making the most of the moments that matter?*

In addition to these questions, and many more, it was the beginning of the end of my twenty-year marriage. And, my professional role at the time was new, controversial, challenging, and not supported by most of my peers and colleagues. I faced major adversity at work and in life. This certainly provided the major blow that hurt everywhere.

What am I going to do? Where do I begin? How am I going to deal with all of this? One step at a time!

In the following weeks, months, and ultimately for the rest of my life, I made the commitment to learn more about me, my values, my needs, my beliefs and limited beliefs, what was motivating me, and what was holding me back. The more I discovered the more I was aware; the more I was aware, the more choices I had; with the better choices I had, the better life that I desired was created. This book will cover some of the tools, tips, and resources that helped me and many others along the way.

My twenty-five plus years in the corporate environment was the equivalent of an associate's degree, undergraduate degree, MBA, and PhD—just through the experience of my career. I was so fortunate not to know better at times, and did not let what I didn't know stop me from going after what I wanted, no matter what. I did not place limitations on myself when it came to advancing my career and financial freedom. **I did not know what I did not know until I knew it,** and only then did I make different choices.

My unawareness of the differences between men and women regarding opportunities in the workplace actually helped me ask for what had not been asked for before … who knew? Equality was always a state of mind and a matter of fact for me. Yes, I did face adversity often, but that provided personal power and fuel to go after a different outcome. I was successful most of the time. There was also a price to pay along this juncture, and without the help of a few good mentors, and a sponsor in the right place at the right time, my career path would have been very different. We will talk more about the absolute benefits of attracting and cultivating mentors and sponsors for advancement in work and life. (See the mentor/sponsor section in Chapter Three.)

I feel very fortunate to have had the opportunity to work for, with, and against mostly men during my career. There were definitely times when it was difficult, and felt unfair or isolating, yet it also provided the opportunity to take calculated (and some not so) risks

INTRODUCTION

to get ahead. For me, many of the opportunities I went after had not been attempted before ... there was nothing to measure against, therefore anything I did would be new and different. I looked for them and seized them often. Because most of the time the company or leader had nothing to lose, I asked for monetary rewards associated with the risk and got them! Often it was one-and-done negotiation—until the next time when there was an opportunity to once again negotiate for more!

What I was not aware of until well after leaving the corporate environment was how "fight" was natural for a man and "fight, flight, or freeze" mode was unnatural and detrimental for a woman who was always in this state. Fight, flight, or freeze are stress triggers that are hardwired in our brains to respond to a real or perceived threat or danger. It is an automatic response that prepares the body to "fight" from perceived attack, harm, or threat to our survival. Until I discovered this, I was not aware of what being "feminine" or "masculine" was, or why it mattered. This new awareness led me on the path of discovery and a deeper understanding of the gender differences at the social, emotional, and physical—or neuroscience—levels.

There is some fascinating brain research on gender differences that is worth exploring in this book, and we will talk about the Gender Partnership and why it is crucial to the future of business and the economy, and of course one's personal power, in Chapter Three.

Fast forward to 2008. After twenty-eight years in California I relocated back to Boston and once again restarted my business of speaking, coaching, and consulting—helping with the advancement of women, and a few good men, to help them discover and bring their authentic leadership style through the power of their voice and choice.

Have you ever experienced the "Imposter Syndrome?" Well, that was me! A speaker? Really, with my voice and limitations and the struggle to be heard! It was so frustrating to have a deep desire to share, and the greater fear of not being heard. It was an emotional and physical challenge.

In 2010, I was watching television—something I hardly ever do—when a preview for *The Dr. OZ Show* on the topic of "Your Voice Could Be Killing You," and it caught my attention. I watched it filled with tears, emotions, and hope that someone could either tell me there was something wrong and if it could or could not be fixed. After all the years of voice coaching, toast masters, etc., nothing was changing the outcome of my voice limitations.

Immediately, I found a specialist here in Boston and went to see him. He walked in the room (and I have to say, he was not too bad on the eyes), and when I introduced myself he said, "Oh my, what have we here? We definitely need to do something about this."

"What do you mean?" I asked.

He said, "You have such a strong presence, and a little girl voice ... they don't go together!" After testing he went on to say that he had good news and bad news. The bad news was I had a paralyzed vocal cord, and the good news was he could fix it! He highly urged me to do this, and said that if I was his sister, he would insist on it. I asked him if he liked his sister! We both laughed, and I went in for surgery on December 29, 2010. I woke up with NO voice. Needless to say, the past seemed to be dictating my future, but it was temporary. After a few months the voice emerged, still soft, but much stronger.

I got my voice back in so many ways, not just in volume, but in confidence, freedom, and truly being present and in the moment without the handicap of voice limitation. Life begins every day, and this surely was more impactful than ever after the surgery.

So many people have encouraged me to share my insight, knowledge, and wisdom with others that may feel stuck, uninspired, at a turning point in their life and wondering, "Is this all there is to life?" The answer is a resounding: NO! What I have learned over many years of personal and professional development and growth is that we already have what it takes inside to design, develop, and create a more meaningful life, and if I can share one or more things that helps you toward that direction, then I am fulfilling a personal passion and purpose.

Lastly, what is near and dear to my heart is helping you find YOUR Voice, how you are heard; YOUR Brand, how you are seen; and YOUR Presence, how you are remembered in the world. I am all about "paying it forward," and I hope you will be too.

Chapter One

Building Your A-Game

Be seen — Be heard — Be remembered!

Everything starts with you! Think about it; once you choose to be conscious and aware of anything and everything around you … there is not one thing in life that isn't connected to you. Now, does that mean you need to know everything? What is "everything"? Everything, to each of us, is individual and unlimited, based on our personal desires to discover new knowledge and insights. We have the power of free will and choice in regard to how we want to handle any situation. What is important is how we use our personal power, professional presence, responsibility, accountability, and actions in our daily lives.

My intention for this book is simply to create awareness for you in areas that you may not have been thinking about or have forgotten about. Use this book as a gentle reminder, and more importantly, to think about what it is you want or desire in your life and how to go about creating it.

About a year ago I woke up around three thirty in the morning with a need to write down what I had just been dreaming about, and before I knew it the clock said 5:34 a.m.... what? And more importantly, my reaction to what I saw in front of me was, "Whoa! What is this?" Seriously, I had a manila file folder (the only thing handy in the middle of the night) and saw all of these key words written all over the front cover. Inside the cover was the diagram below.

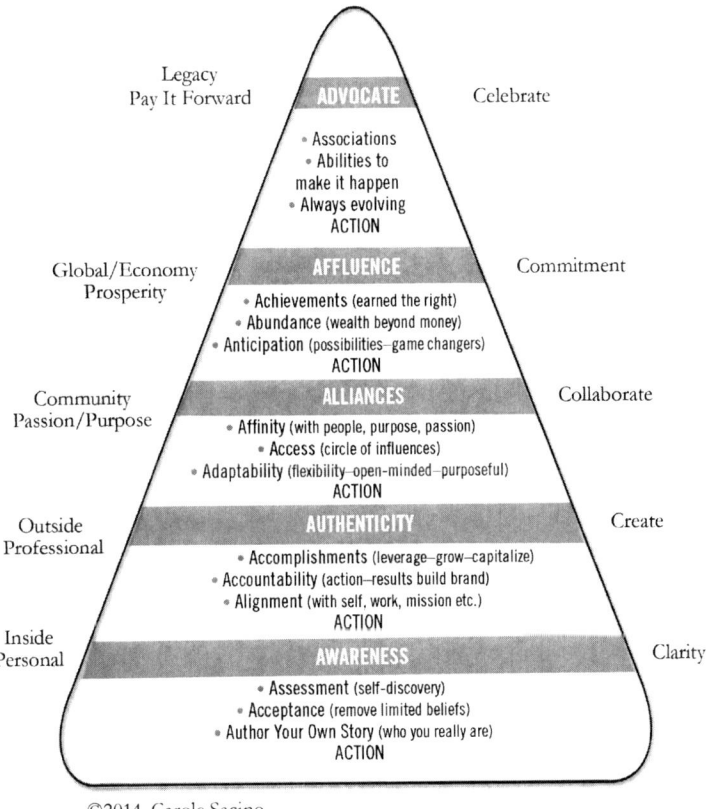

I decided to go get at least an hour of sleep before trying to really understand what all of this meant. But I was so interested in what I wrote I actually could not go to sleep. I decided to get back up and start linking all the pieces together, and what emerged were the concepts for how to build your A-Game in work and life. And screaming at me was the idea of how to "be seen, be heard, and be remembered!" I worked on this for a few days and was totally in the flow—when everything is effortless—during that creative process.

Then I let my head get in the way, telling myself that what was unfolding here wasn't any big deal, and someone had probably already done this anyway! Even though I was feeling this way, something bigger than my logic was moving me to trusting myself to share this idea of the book! I took the bold step of sharing this folder, writing, and thoughts with a friend over coffee, waiting for her to validate that, "It's nice, but not unique." Instead, I got an overwhelming endorsement to move forward with this concept for a book. And a cautionary note, "You shouldn't share this with too many, someone is likely to steal your idea." When she told me this I immediately thought about "scarcity." Have you heard the saying the glass is either half empty or half full? *Scarcity* would be the half-empty feeling; a sense of lacking, limitations, uncertainty, shortage, and more risk averse for fear of not having enough.

My next immediate thought was about "abundance"—more than enough for all.

Abundance is the concept of "the glass is half full" and ready for more. It is a sense of fullness, plenitude, certainty, positivity, affluence, wealth (not just money but resources), and calculated risk-taking without fear. Abundance is about unlimited resources, and there is more than enough for everyone.

I had been told over the years that I was way too optimistic and was not dealing with reality. "Just look around," my friends would say. "The economy is in the tank," and, "We are going to hell in a hand basket," and of course the, "You should save your money for a rainy day; you never know what could happen." Yet, I believed then and I still believe today that what we focus on grows bigger.

If I focused on abundance, feeling that life offered more than enough for everyone, then I did not need to feel doom and gloom. And when I was in sales, everything was competitive internally and externally, and quite frankly it was exhausting to always be operating from the scarcity mindset. I have the ability, as do you, to reframe any thought, belief, or feeling anyway you desire, and my choice is reframe "scarcity" to "abundance."

Growing up in a one-paycheck, large-family environment, we were expected to earn our keep and contribute to the household. I started working more than one job at the age of thirteen. I had to pay at least ten percent of my earnings back into the house and began to buy my own clothes. My family came from a scarcity mindset, but as a result of earning money early on I felt abundantly full and confident that I would not live in lack. The funny thing was even when I didn't have very much no one ever knew it, and my dad always thought I had a stash of money in the bank. I never did try to change his or anyone's mind.

So after the endorsement from my friend, I began stepping out and taking a few more calculated risks. I shared the concept with a few professional associates and experts in the field of leadership, and got an overwhelming endorsement to bring the book forward.

I came to the realization that this book idea was not about me, it was about the giving of me to others. Being all about giving, sharing, and supporting by helping one person, or many, to create the lives they desire, I would bring this book out! My life has been enriched with so many opportunities to seek the many gifts of life experience, deeper insight, and awareness. I have a deep passion and purpose to connect and communicate with others in a different, more vulnerable way through my personal stories.

I said yes to bringing the book out and immediately went into "freeze" mode. I could not write a single word and found myself stuck and not knowing where to begin. And part of the process of getting to the stage of writing helped me to realize that this is part of the story I need to talk about in the book. It does not matter how much personal and professional development we do, there is always a challenge in life for us to go deeper in dealing with our limited beliefs, self-doubt, and self-sabotaging experiences.

Another "aha" moment and, another gift for me to experience yet again, was to be able to get past the wall of resistance, live with fear and vulnerability, and share it with the reader. This book was written in real time, and I trust that what was meant to be shared came through in these pages.

There's always work to be done! Each phase of growth starts the process over again. Every change we face gives us the opportunity to pause and choose what we want to do or not to do. When we get the inner voice urging us to take action and we don't listen, it does not go away; it comes back another day until we move where it is guiding us.

The entire book is about awareness and authenticity! Whether it is personal power, professional presence and brand, tapping into our passion or purpose, or creating prosperity! And, how to leverage more in work and life that helps create your authentic voice.

Awareness—From the Inside Out!

It's personal! My favorite saying and a personal driver in my life is, **"You don't know what you don't know until you know it, and only then can you to do something about it."** We often are running on autopilot; going through life accepting what is until it no longer is working for us, right? Sometimes we get triggered by something or someone and cannot quite figure out why we had the reaction we had.

Throughout this book you will be asked to think about something at a deeper level and take a personal look inside yourself. How much do you know about yourself? Are you satisfied with how things are going for you in work and life? Are there any changes you'd like to make? **Awareness precedes action every time** and here's a great place to start.

Chapter Two: Awareness will take you on a self-discovery tour to gain clarity about your conscious and unconscious behaviors that are driven by your core values, personal needs, natural talents, intuition, and energy! And then there are those limited beliefs that tend to get in your way, leading you to believe you have no choice. I am here to share that there ALWAYS is a choice. We will explore ways to see, feel, and think differently—it's a matter of recording over the old and creating new thoughts and behaviors through action steps to get you there.

Authentic Leadership

Professional presence and brand is YOU! It's not your job title, function, or where you work. It's creating the brand you want people to remember. Designing your brand for the world to see comes from knowing and living your authentic self no matter what. Do you know what people would say about you today? If so, does it align with who you feel you are? Or is there work to be done to make that happen?

Chapter Three: Authenticity will explore how you are showing up, who you know, who knows you, and what do they know or say about you. We will explore what sits under the political umbrella and why it matters. You will learn assessment methods that help you make clear decisions in all areas of life. You will discover how authenticity and influence go hand in hand. You will see how and what we communicate affects how you are to **be seen, be heard, and be remembered**. We will explore why mentors and sponsors are key components to advancement in organizations. And you will gain insight into the power of effective networking as a means of enhancing your personal and professional presence in work and life.

Alliances/Common-Unity

Who do you know, who knows you, and why do they want to know you? How do you establish a rapport and leverage these alliances for something bigger than yourself? Think about what you are passionate about—do the people in your life align with your passion? Are you purposeful in your association with causes, events, mission, and people that move you forward with ease?

Who we align with speaks volumes about who we are without saying a word. People unconsciously and consciously make judgments based on what they see. Being mindful and purposeful keeps you in charge of your brand.

Chapter Four: Alliances/Common-Unity will explore the intrinsic motivation for being in community and how it moves us forward into action around something meaningful and valuable in our lives. We are fueled by connections and collaboration in work and life, and the affinity with like-minded people is what we always are seeking in life. This chapter will help explore our passion and purpose, and why we get involved and when we should expand and grow our affinity groups. We'll discuss how to access and leverage our circle of influences from a place of collaboration—creating win/win/win scenarios in work and life.

Affluence

What's driving our economy? Who is driving the new economy, and what is your role in it? How do you leverage what you bring to the table? We've moved into a "she" change and the future is dependent on the feminine wisdom and role we play in the world. How do we stay current, connect, and collaborate more for greater impact in work and life?

In Chapter Five: Affluence, we will take a look at economy as an exchange of something that creates abundance and prosperity in our lives. The data shows that women are the new economy, but are we making the most of this opportunity? How do you "ASK" for and negotiate more effectively for what you want in a more confidant manner? If you can anticipate and adapt to the changing economy by conscious choice you are more able to adjust from a place of self-confidence versus fear.

Advocate

Leave a legacy by paying it forward! Has someone advocated on your behalf in the past? If so, how did it make you feel? Has there been a time when you wanted to advocate a cause and stopped out of fear, or a lack or limited belief that you weren't qualified? There are so many others who will benefit from YOU being YOU!

In Chapter Six: Advocate, it is time to pause, reflect, and celebrate—it's your time! There comes a time and place in our lives when life has granted us gifts such as awareness, knowledge, and insight and that offer us huge opportunities to expand, grow, and evolve on our journey called life. And it is time to pay it forward to others. You have the ability to make this happen, the personal power to drive results, and the professional presence and brand to align and collaborate with passion and purpose. One's legacy is all about clarity, connection, commitment, collaboration, and celebration with others on their journey of life.

Time to activate it!

Chapter Two

Awareness

Until "unconscious" becomes "conscious" we are in the dark, and awareness is the first step in this process of building your A-Game. The rest of this book is designed to constantly be creating awareness of what could be valuable for you in designing your authentic life.

The Brain in Mind

Your brain is the organ of your personality, character, and intelligence and is heavily involved with making you who you are.
—Daniel Amen, author

I wanted to include something about Neuro-Leadership and Emotional Intelligence in this book for several reasons. It is a new and expanding field of endless possibilities, and without awareness and knowledge of them, we cannot succeed in business and life with any sustainability. Why do I say this? Read on as I share points of view based on the experts and research from their books and talks. Again, my intention here is to help create awareness about this ever-expanding opportunity to change and created the lives we desire, and to learn how to **be seen, be heard and be remembered** in a new and impactful way.

David Rock, founding president of The Neuroscience Institute and expert author of many publications including *Your Brain at Work* and *Quiet Leadership*, has made all of this neuroscience accessible and easy to understand. His recent special report, "Managing with the Brain in Mind," featured in booz&co.'s *strategy+business* magazine, is a great way to introduce this topic.

Neuroscience has discovered that the brain is highly flexible and able to change patterns and processes. Neural connections can be reformed, new behaviors can be learned, and even the most entrenched behaviors can be modified at any age—indicating we are capable of changing our minds, literally. How cool is that?

Rock states, "Research indicates there is a reason to believe emotion, more than intellectual ability, drives a leader's thinking in decision making and in interpersonal relationships." An effective leader has the ability to perceive, identify, understand, and successfully manage emotions, and, the emotions of others.

Consider these questions about leaders:

› *Have you ever worked for or with someone who demonstrates these characteristics?*
› *How did it feel to work with them?*
› *Or have you worked for or with someone who did not display empathy or understanding?*
› *How did that feel?*

The brain will make the shift only when it is engaged in mindful attention. Rock shows us that mindfulness is the key that provides all of us with greater personal control over negative emotions and stress, while helping us to enhance our well-being. When we are present and in the moment and mindful of our intentions for change, the chances are extremely favorable to sustain lasting results.

In other words, without being in a state of mindfulness, intention, attention, and action, achieving our goals or desired outcomes becomes impossible. There are classes for mindfulness training popping up all over corporate America, and likely in a town near you. These types of programs were once viewed as "nice to have" classes—to offer along with leadership development programs—and now are becoming more of a "need to have" as people shift toward meaningful engagement at work and in life.

The saying "seeing is believing" is often really "believing is seeing," and what you say may not be what others are hearing! Your brain responds to what is seen and felt, and then it becomes your belief. Think about that for a moment. How we are seen by others actually creates an imprint as a belief! An example would be: *I see a positive person that always has a smile on their face. I have now imprinted the belief that she/he is always happy and I like that.* The importance of nonverbal communication such as this, and how it shapes the belief in the minds of others, is something to remain mindful of throughout this book.

Brain on Autopilot

When your attention is diverted by a threat, perceived or real, it cannot move into self-discovery or any action at all. Basically, your brain is in a lockdown mode until it feels safe. The following explains a few basics of what actually is happening with your brain.

"The human brain is a social organ. Its physiological and neurological reactions are directly and profoundly shaped by social interaction and the brain experiences the workplace first and foremost as a social system," reports David Rock. An example given in "Managing with the Brain in Mind" discusses how a person feels reprimanded when asked to do an assignment that seems unworthy, or is told to take a pay cut. This feeling actually is experienced as a neural impulse and is as powerful and painful as a blow to the head.

CHAPTER TWO: AWARENESS

I have felt this two-by-four many times. The reaction I experience is on autopilot and comes from deep down inside, and I can't quite explain it when it's happening. Next time you are triggered, pause, reflect, and become mindful about what the brain is trained to do and choose how you want to move forward. "Most people who work in companies learn to rationalize or temper their reactions; they 'suck it up' as the common parlance puts it. But they also limit their commitment and engagement," Rock tells us. Sound familiar?

Research shows the social brain starts with the "threat and reward" response as a neurological mechanism that governs human behavior. An example would be when you encounter something unexpected, like seeing a car crossing over into your lane out of the corner of your eye. The limbic system (the primitive part of the brain common to many animals) is aroused. It is called the "fundamental organizing principle of the brain."

When this happens (it is in milliseconds) neurons are activated and begin to fire on cylinders seeking the threat or reward. If there is a threat, it triggers the amygdala that hijacks the remainder of our brain and releases the hormone cortisol, and puts us into a state of "fight, flight, or freeze" until the threat has been eliminated. When there is no immediate threat the amygdala is in the background scanning for any potential threats as part of its natural function.

In addition to governing our reactive behavior, the brain oversees our social behaviors. And when a person is engaged they are attracted to and inspired by and committed to their work and relationships. The sense of belonging is at the core of human spirit. And collaborating and bonding with others makes us the happiest.

Have you ever felt an instant connection with someone from a place of ease familiarity? Here is one reason why this happens for us.

In our brains there are "mirror neurons." These neurons fire when we perform an action or see another perform an action; in a sense the neuron "mirrors" the behavior of another person as though the observer were performing the action of the observed person. It helps the brain to understand the actions and intentions of other people and their actions. For example, you're watching a football game on television, and the quarterback takes a big hit from a defensive lineman twice his size. You automatically cringe, or recoil in your chair, and even suck in your breath. This reaction is thought to be the result of mirror neurons. When I became aware of this I thought it was interesting to know and, more so, to observe it when it was happening. It has to move from running on autopilot in the background of our brain to conscious awareness.

"Every action or decision either supports or undermines perceived level of Status, Certainty, Autonomy, Relatedness, and Fairness among followers," also known as SCARF, by David Rock.

Status and Its Discontents

We always are looking at how social encounters either enhance or diminish one's status. (I call it Comparison Cathy.)

We are biologically programmed to care about status because it favors our survival. I found this new awareness and understanding helped me to reframe some of my limited beliefs about certain situations or people. Knowing it is a function of the brain, and now realizing how I can move into conscious creation about what I want instead, developed a sense of personal power for me.

I remember growing up in a large family when the entertainment included playing cards and board games, especially Monopoly. When you think about the object of the game, it requires strategy, risk, money, luck, and negotiation if you want to win, right? There are players that give up early by buying everything and they run out of money, or players that strategically buy and then trade for advantage, and those strategic buyers that load up with houses and motels.

And then there are those players who are determined to win no matter what. They stay in the game using every last dollar and mortgaging their properties and finally have no choice—game over. This is a great example of "Status" from the SCARF model in action.

Personally, I buy and load and focus on winning the game no matter who is playing. Sometimes how we play the game mirrors how we play in life. Consciously or unconsciously, it is part of our internal landscape and shapes us at many levels.

Craving Certainty

We all have a craving for certainty, and when we encounter familiarity our brain shifts to an autopilot mode that consists of hard-wired neural connections. Autopilot makes it easy to do things such as talking while driving or listening to music. But the minute the brain registers ambiguity or confusion it flashes an error signal and implements the threat arousal—you must pay full attention to the situation. To use the driving example, the trigger would be that you may have missed your exit and didn't notice because you were in your autopilot zone.

How many times a day does this happen? For me, driving these days, I am in a constant state of alertness. I will be driving and run into heavy traffic, and I immediately shut off the radio and all conversations, and go into full concentration mode until it feels safe again.

Uncertainty registers an error, gap, or tension that something needs our attention and correction before we are comfortable again. Mild uncertainty gets our attention and also increases adrenalin and levels of dopamine enough to spark curiosity and move people to make changes. This is when adrenalin is good for us!

I personally choose to stay in a mildly uncertain place that stimulates my natural curiosity and keeps me in the present moment at all times.

All of life is uncertain—it is the perception of too much uncertainty that undercuts focus and performance. Think about it, if we are always worrying about when the next shoe is going to drop we will be in a constant state of fight, flight, or freeze. Awareness precedes action and choice. Pause and reflect on what and why you are feeling a sense of uncertainty and ask yourself: If it was more certain then what actions would I take? If it is a situation you can't personally change, then ask yourself: What can I do to make it work for me given the current situation?

Autonomy

As long as people feel they can execute their own decisions without much oversight, stress remains under control. The human brain has evolved in response to stressors for thousands of years, and has attuned at the unconscious level to the ways in which social encounters threaten or support our capacity for choice, according to Rock.

For example, your boss asks you to come up with a strategic business plan for the design and launch of a new product line because you are the best at this type of thinking. You now want the autonomy to execute it with full confidence from your boss—eliminating unnecessary stress in the meantime.

When there is a perception of reduced autonomy, such as being micromanaged on the assignment, a threat response easily could be generated. When one experiences a lack of control, or the perception of uncertainty, this further raises one's stress levels. By contrast, greater autonomy or the perception of it increases the levels of certainty and reduces stress. People are far more effective and engaged when there is a level of certainty and autonomy in their work and life.

I have not always been aware of it, but throughout the years I always was looking for more autonomy in my life, and it was another reason I chose sales as a profession. It gave me a sense of certainty, mild uncertainty, freedom, and control over my decisions. When I was in a place of certainty my self-confidence levels were stronger and I made better choices.

Presenting options allows for self and others to organize their schedules and priorities to get the work done in a less stressful way, and when given more control over decision-making, the perception of autonomy is all that matters.

Relating to Relatedness

Collaboration requires trust and empathy in the relationship. Yet the brain's ability to feel trust and empathy about others is shaped by whether they are perceived to be in the same social group. Examples can include what school you attended (Ivy League or community college), or to what organizations you belong (in the inner circle or sitting on the sidelines), or in which community you live (high-rent district or inner-city housing). Again, our autopilot moves us into relatedness (and I would also include unconscious bias) as another way of viewing this action.

"Each time a person meets someone new, the brain automatically makes quick friend-or-foe distinctions and then experiences them in ways that are colored by those distinctions. When the new person is perceived as different, the information travels along the neural pathways that are associated with uncomfortable feelings," Rock shares.

Leaders who understand this will find many ways to apply it, as in the case of team dynamics. There must be deliberate intentions of putting people together in teams in a way to minimize the potential threat response. Oh, if the leaders I worked with knew then what is known by us today, life would have been far more rewarding, productive, and purposeful. And if I knew this when leading teams, I could have avoided hostile group dynamics, people resigning, and stressful dialog and decisions. That said, it takes an individual contributor to begin the chain of change.

We cannot assume trust or mandate it, nor can we compel empathy or goodwill or automatically expect it of others. A relationship needs to be formed before we can go there. These qualities develop when people's brains start to recognize former strangers as friends. This often requires time and repeated social interaction. Think about the recent relationships you established in work or life. Take a few minutes to review the dynamics of how and why these relationships are what they are today. It will be a good exercise in helping with building the awareness muscle.

This is something to be mindful of as you build your entourage and expand your network of connections.

When people make a strong social connection, their brain begins to secrete the hormone oxytocin—a chemical linked with affection, maternal behavior, sexual arousal, generosity, and connectedness. This disarms the threat response and helps to build a sense of confidence, collaboration, and creativity with ease and grace. I cover more on this in Chapter Three: Authenticity.

Playing for Fairness

Rock talks about fairness as "the perception that an event has been unfair generates a strong response in the limbic system, stirring hostility and undermining trust. As with status, people perceive fairness in relative terms, feeling more satisfied with fair exchange that offers a minimal reward than an unfair exchange in which the reward is substantial."

How many of you have experienced this in work or life? What was your response to it when it happened and what did you do about it? Personally, this was a significant driver in my decision making, and I also relate this to my deep commitment to my principles based on core values. I was a VP of sales and was asked to pull together a golf tournament for the CEO and vice presidents of my division and our key customers. *Wait a minute—I am a Vice President, the only woman, and excluded from the Boy's Club and asked to do this?* Not fair, not right, and not happening. Of course, I could not say no to the CEO, so what I did instead was set a foursome of women to play in the tournament, and I would be playing golf. That would have been fine, except I really didn't know how to play golf.

When I shared the news about having a female group of golfers with my boss he was taken aback, and I said, "I have the shoes, the bag, and the balls," and he followed up with, "Yes, you do!" Now this was pure principle taking over here, and not really a smart decision. I went for it anyway.

CHAPTER TWO: AWARENESS

The three other ladies canceled because they were intimidated by the other people playing, and there I was, the only woman. I didn't even know all the golf etiquette, but I knew just enough to be dangerous. My boss, with a smirk on his face, asked me to lead the way ... what!? I was facing the lake in a golf cart I have never driven. Not knowing there was a reverse key, I accelerate forward and missed going in the lake by inches. EVERYBODY was watching us and I turned and said, "Just kidding!"

I silently prayed as we approached the hole and my boss said, "Ladies first." Again, WHAT!? So I stepped up to the tee, placed the ball, took a practice swing, then put my head down and hit the ball. It connected and moved—not far, but at least I made the connection. The rest of the day was far more relaxing, and everything turned out okay being with my customers that were totally enjoying the events of the day. Even though I experienced fear, doubt, and uncertainty, I also felt that using my voice and expecting "fairness" was the right thing to do. I set the example for others in the future.

"The cognitive need for fairness is so strong that people are willing to fight or die for causes they believe are just or commit themselves wholeheartedly to an organization or cause they recognize as fair," says Rock.

The old boys' network is a great example that those who are not part of it always perceive it as fundamentally unfair. I was constantly up against this very issue, and at times it potentially became a professional derailment ... as in the story I shared.

Like certainty, fairness is served by transparency. People who share information in a timely manner can help keep others engaged and motivated. An example would be when an organization must make staff reductions for business reasons. Morale is favorable when there is a sense of fairness that not one group is the target and reductions are fairly dispersed across the organization. On the flip side if there is a lack of communication, empathy, and trust strategically executed with all employees in mind, then doubt and uncertainty take over. Humans cannot think creatively, work well with others, or make informed decisions when their threat responses are on high alert. We will discuss ways to minimize this in the Energy section below.

The SCARF model provides a means of bringing conscious awareness to what we all experience in life. It helps alert you to people's core concerns (which they may not even understand themselves), and gives us another way we can calibrate our thoughts (status being affected), feelings (autonomy or fairness), words (relatedness), and actions (craving for certainty) for a more purposeful outcome.

This field of neuro-leadership and neuroscience is evolving daily, and research is discovering endless possibilities and potential for a better human experience. It's an exciting time to know that no matter what we are today, opportunity for growth and expansion is available to each of us when we are ready to make a shift.

Energy

Until you make the unconscious conscious, it will direct your life and you will call it fate.
—C. G. Jung, Swiss psychologist

It is up to each of us to embrace the stages of learning in order to capitalize on this process, shorten the time of real change in one's life and be more open, present, and available to be curious about what you don't already know! This small shift alone opens up endless possibilities to become a more interested and interesting person. When you come from a place of curiosity the energy level you are in attracts others to you! Good, bad, or indifferent. You may be scratching your head saying, "What is she talking about?"

I had no conscious thought about energy—let alone understanding that most of what we experience in life is operating in the unconscious mind. Curious as usual, I wanted to understand more about the conscious and unconscious mind and how it affected our daily lives. I discovered Maslow's work, among others, and share some of this with you here in this chapter.

Psychologist Abraham Maslow's The Four Stages of Learning!

Unconscious-incompetence—not aware. You don't know what you don't know and you must become conscious of this before creating awareness (naïve stage).

Conscious-incompetence—you become aware, have a realization about your actions and commit to learn (discovery stage).

Conscious-competent—you achieve a skill and you can perform it reliably at will (effort stage).

Unconscious-competent—you are so practiced the skill enters into the unconscious part of the brain (instincts stage).

This is the basis for creating awareness and active change in the areas of life with intention, attention, and action. We will circle back to this from time to time within the book.

Energy—Where It All Begins!
Let's talk about energy! Over 100 years ago Albert Einstein addressed the scientific community, passionately presenting the idea that everything we see, hear, taste, touch, and smell is not matter, but energy. **Everything that "matters" is energy.** He went on to say that energy cannot be created or destroyed, it only can be transformed.

Bob Procter, the best-selling author of *You Were Born Rich,* and a featured guest in the movie *The Secret,* has been helping millions with his teachings and stories for more than forty years. Here's what he has to say about energy:

"Everything in our universe constantly vibrates and moves. Both the nonphysical and the physical aspects of our universe are made up of energy and intelligence that vibrates or, in other words, oscillates, resonates, pulsates. Nothing rests. The difference between the physical and nonphysical is the rate of vibration."

This law is responsible for the difference between what we can see with our naked eye, like our hands, for example, and that which we cannot see but is there, like a radio wave.

We are energetic beings; always in motion and vibrating at various frequencies throughout the day, and this is driven by our conscious and unconscious thoughts, feelings, and actions. **What we think about comes about,** and it is possible to shift your energy field by just by changing your thoughts and beliefs.

When I first heard about all of this, it instantly created enthusiasm and passion—to know that the power of thought can change everything, and I could not wait to dig in deeper, learn more, and most definitely apply it in my life. Being someone that is always looking for a *win/win/win*—an "everyone wins" outcome—this provided a great platform from which to create a more robust relationship with my friends, family, work, community, and the endless possibilities I could create in my life.

At first I thought ... *it's a little woo-woo,* and I was a buttoned-up, practical, senior-level executive that was embracing this, yet was not comfortable talking about it. Actually, it was more fun to act on this knowledge and insight without sharing it with others and have them wonder why I was different and what had shifted in me!

What I also experienced were easier conversations, ease and flow with decisions, and getting results in all facets of my life. I

CHAPTER TWO: AWARENESS

felt lighter and more energetic, and was open and available in the moment always.

I mentioned **we don't know what we don't know until we know it**; back in 2007 I was reading *Harvard Business Review* and the lead story was "Manage Your Energy, Not Your Time" by Tony Schwartz and Catherine McCarthy. Perfect, it was a topic that was reaching the halls of corporate America, leading to a discussion in the C-Suite, and becoming a new way of transforming business. "The science of stamina has advanced to the point where individuals, teams and whole organizations can, with some straightforward interventions, significantly increase their capacity to get things done." Okay, it was slow to take hold, and still remains this way today, but let's face it—any change in this environment that helps us as individuals to be more aware and in control of our destiny is positive.

Here are several key call-outs from the article worth sharing, and I will blend in my point of view along the way.

1. "The core problem with working longer hours is that time is a finite resource." If energy is what we are and it cannot be created or destroyed … how do we redeploy it to work to our advantage? "Defined in physics as the capacity to work, energy comes from four main wellsprings in human beings: the body, emotions, mind and spirit."

2. "To effectively reenergize their workforces, organizations need to shift their emphasis from getting more out of people to investing more in them, so they are motivated and are able to bring more of themselves to work every day." It is great if organizations do in fact step up and do this, but we cannot expect them to do for us what we can do for ourselves. Bringing the personal power back to where it belongs—with you!

3. "To recharge themselves, individuals need to recognize the cost of energy-depleting behaviors and then take

responsibility to change them regardless of the circumstances they're facing." I have found that awareness of limited self-talk and changing it is the quickest way to recharge.

If you want to read the article in full go to www.hbr.org. Throughout this book I will give it my voice and share it through personal experiences or stories in which it has been demonstrated in work and life for me.

Energy Management

Energy is always in motion, and we experience it differently depending on what is happening in our lives. Energy cannot be created or destroyed, only managed, and we experience energy at the physical, emotional, and mental levels. Here's a more detailed look at each level. Below is a breakdown of the different types of energy and how we can navigate and manage our energy levels by choice.

Physical energy. It is important to take care of replenishing your energy levels throughout the day. Reducing stress by taking breaks to reenergize is so valuable and does wonders for creativity and response levels. Become aware of the signs of imminent energy loss including restlessness, yawning, hunger, and difficulty concentrating. Step away from your desk at 90- to 120-minute intervals throughout the day.

I find that a glass of water prevents me from following the hunger signs to the snack shop and helps more often than not. For those times when you really need to eat something, prepare small, light snacks that give you fulfillment without too many calories, and eat every few hours to keep your energy levels balanced.

Emotional energy. Defuse negative emotions such as irritability, impatience, anxiety, and insecurity through deep abdominal breathing. Also I will find a picture, a tree, or something to focus on that brings me joy and that raises my energy level. It will defuse the frustration, and give me the opportunity to pause, reflect, and decide how I want this situation to go for me.

CHAPTER TWO: AWARENESS

Infuse positive emotions in yourself and others by expressing appreciation and gratitude through conversation whether digital, verbal, or written. Acknowledgment is a powerful tool that is easy to use. Ladies, when someone acknowledges you, please accept it by saying "thank you"! We tend to downplay ourselves when compliments come our way and say things like, "Oh, it was nothing," or go on to justify why we did what we did. It is a disempowering move and does not serve anyone when it happens.

Mental energy. Find the time that works best for you and step away from e-mail, phones, and meetings whenever possible. For me, the mornings are my most energetic and creative times of the day. I have a ritual of doing all the important tasks early before the day starts for most people. I continually try to discipline myself (yes, I said try, because it is an ongoing struggle to maintain) to not jump on e-mail or any of the social media sites before I complete my list. When I do jump on the social media sites time escapes me, and then I am frustrated with myself for not honoring my commitment. It is a constant reminder that we are always on the journey of self-discovery, self-awareness, and self-acceptance.

Let others know that you are unavailable and will return e-mails at a specific time of the day. When I was on a deadline or had a "do not disturb" frame of mind, I often did not share this with others and assumed they would know or understand. Wrong! You need to set expectations for others—they cannot read your mind. An example would be an out-of-office e-mail message that says, "If there is an emergency, then please call me directly." It is amazing how fast people acclimate to these new expectations.

What I found was much of the trivial information that comes across the wire does not require the personal attention of a response. The more you respond, the more involved, the more it's now on your plate. Have you heard the saying, "How do I get the monkey off my back?" It's a way of delegating more effectively. Monkeys are a metaphor for taking the initiative on tasks and responsibilities. So when you dialog with others someone always has the "monkey on their back." Once I became aware of this and observed it in conversations, either personally or otherwise, it was by choice what monkey I let stay on my back. Next time you are in dialog with others look for how the conversation goes and who ends up being responsible to take the next step. If it makes sense to take it on yourself, then agree to it, and if you feel it should be the responsibility of the other person be sure that is clearly communicated before the conversation is completed. I have saved myself many hours of frustration and unnecessary worry and anxiety over things that ultimately did not belong to me just by being clear with my expectations.

I am big on "to-do" lists and use them as a reminder of my priorities for the day. There is a danger with "to-do" lists as a measurement of what needs to be done and what did not get done. Many people I coach have a guilty feeling when they do not meet everything on the list! As we explore deeper and learn that the lists are beyond reasonable to accomplish in one day, we implement a priority process to ensure completion and personal satisfaction—shifting the negative to a positive and making room for other things that replenish the energy levels throughout the day.

Spiritual energy. Identify your "sweet spot"—activities that give you the feeling of effortlessness, effectiveness, and fulfillment. Add more of these moments into your life by design. When it is effortless you are tapping into your natural talents, needs, values, and what we call "being in the flow."

According to Milhaly Csikszentmihlyi, psychologist and author of the book *FLOW, The Psychology of Optimal Experiences*, flow is the mental state of operation in which a person performing an activity is fully immersed in a feeling of energized focus, full involvement, and enjoyment in the process of the activity. In essence, flow is characterized by complete absorption in what one does.

Other colloquial terms include: to be in the moment, on a roll, on fire, in tune, or singularly focused.

› When was the last time you felt in the flow?
› What were you doing at the time?
› How can you bring more flow into your life?

How Do You Start Your Day?

Repeat anything often enough and it will start to become you.
—Tom Hopkins, sales expert trainer/speaker

Affirmations! In order to change your belief system you need to reprogram with a new belief system, and this can be done using affirmations—or "I AM" statements—along with the importance of rituals.

Take a minute to think about this; it is a major factor in how your day will go! Rituals are so important, especially when we are committed to our personal journey of growth and expansion. I developed a habit (I believe it takes thirty days to change or incorporate a habit) of gratitude that has totally change my life. An affirmation exercise I use to build this habit every morning before I step out of bed is to write at least five things I am grateful for using the "I am" statement. Example: *I am grateful for my fit, toned, flexible body, and I am grateful for my daughter Jamie and all she brings to the world*. These "I am" statements don't have to be big; it can be as simple as *I am grateful for my health, I am grateful for the ability to tap into creativity*, or *I am grateful to have a great job*. I do this every morning, and sometimes in the evening when I remember, and it not only is a habit … it is a ritual I still do to this day. This practice can be used for any habit you want to create in your life.

It is so important to live your core values, which we talk about in-depth in this book. Affirmations are an activator for your higher-frequency energy levels and it's up to us to clarify priorities, establish rituals, and consciously allocate time, focus, and attention to our desired outcomes in work and life.

Everything has its own vibrational frequency and is a built-in blueprint in our own mind (unconsciously) regarding what is true or not. The blueprint has been designed and sculpted over the years based on what we have experienced, heard, or believed. Sudden or new information is not automatically added. It requires thought, feelings, beliefs, and action to make it happen, and it is stored in our brain's historical database.

There are several high-frequency feelings that raise your vibration: love, generosity, enthusiasm, and happiness. Some high-frequency thoughts and motivations are: creativity, innovation, inspiration, forgiveness, service, and healing.

Here are some of the lower energy feelings, such as sadness, depression, frustration, anger, rage, disillusion, and defeat. Lower-frequency thoughts are: I am not good enough, smart enough, pretty enough, rich enough, or not successful or accomplished.

No matter which way you choose, you will get that result. **What you think about comes about!**

Energy Awareness Assessments

> *The key to growth is the introduction of higher dimensions of consciousness into our awareness.*
> —Lao Tzo, Chinese philosopher

The focus of energy and human spirit is a passion and purpose of mine. So much so that I have certifications in Emotional Intelligence, Energy Leadership, and Motivation Factor, to name a few.

There are two main types of energy awareness assessments: personality and attitudinal. Personality-based assessments, such as Myers Briggs and DISC, are very valuable tools that pinpoint certain personality types so that people can have more of an understanding about what their strengths and weaknesses are. By understanding your personality and how it relates to what you do, you can adapt your behavior to "work with what you have" and to function effectively.

The E.L.I. (Energy Leadership Index) is an attitudinal assessment, which is based on an energy/action model. This assessment differs from personality assessments and is not intended to label a person and have them work well within that label. Instead, it measures your level of energy based on your attitude, or perception and perspective, of your world. Because attitude is subjective, it can be altered. You can alter your attitude and perspective, make a shift in your consciousness, and increase your energy and leadership effectiveness.

As mentioned, I am an assessment junkie. It is fascinating to me how different the assessments are, yet they consistently show similar findings. When I returned home from the Center for Creative Leadership program—a global provider of executive leadership development—I used the feedback and assessment results to create lasting change in my professional and personal life. I would visit the reports a few times a year and do a year-end report of my progress and the impact, delays, detours, and obstacles that continued to get in my way.

Every year people make "resolutions" and goals for what they want to change in the upcoming New Year, and I did something similar for my professional development by asking a series of questions:

› *What new skills do I need to develop?*
› *What new information will help me in leadership development?*
› *What new sales information do I need to incorporate for better results?*
› *What personality or attitudinal trait needs adjustment?*

This was a ritual I did for the last fifteen years while working in corporate America.

What I also discovered was it took many years of creating me, and it would not be an overnight process to change what was not working for me. What I do believe is the intention, attention, and action toward deliberate change happens quickly. And subtle changes may not be painful or distracting you in the moment, yet it's the "toleration" of these changes that still eventually gets in the way. I will cover more of this in this chapter.

Catabolic and Anabolic Energy!

There are two forces that create your world every minute of every day! They are called catabolic and anabolic energy. Let me explain....

On an energetic and cellular level, catabolism usually refers to a breakdown of complex molecules, while anabolism is the opposite. It's a broader statement about destructive and constructive forces in an entire person, who is made up not only of individual cells but also of anabolic and catabolic thoughts and beliefs. The E.L.I. model explains that we have seven different levels of energy, and yet more than 85% of the population surveyed is highly engaged—especially in a work environment—at two levels: Level One L1 energy, also called "Victim Mode" (where everything feels like it is against you), and Level Two L2 energy, also called "Anger Mode" (when you feel mad, frustrated, or attacked), and how this total affects our work environments across the globe.

Anabolic and catabolic energies are predominant in organizations as well as people. Many organizations experience catabolic energy by constantly reacting to their circumstances with worry, fear, doubt, anger, and guilt. And thoughts are indeed contagious. When even a few people in an organization have negative feelings, it can spread like a virus. "Group think" sets in, and their thoughts become group "fact." Once that occurs, the company can implode energetically in a swirl of gossip, negativity, conflict, and contempt.

CHAPTER TWO: AWARENESS

Sadly, many corporate and organizational environments are unhealthy for many of us. I will be sharing information about the quality of energy and how we get to shape it. So many people go through life thinking that they don't have control of their environment and that external world events are shaping their lives. **We don't know what we don't know!** I am here to share with you that positive energy is absolutely available to you here and now and really as simple as being aware of your thoughts, feelings, behavior, and actions, and deciding moment by moment how you want to show up.

Take a moment to think about a situation that made you feel anger. What was happening around you that caused you to feel this way? Do you tend to default to anger when things are not going right? Do you blame others for the situation or outcome? It is natural for most of us to blame others for how we are feeling, because we think it's because of them—when in fact they are triggering something inside of you!

That said, we have the personal power to shift this anytime we want. How, you ask? By asking yourself a series of questions:

What thoughts are roaming through your head and are they justified for this particular scenario? Depending on how you answer, you have the power to reframe your thoughts in a positive way anytime. We talk about this more in Chapter Three: Authenticity.

What behavior are you demonstrating and would you change it if you could? If you are angry, your negative energy levels are being felt by others. If you want a different outcome, it's up to you to make the shift.

What actions are you taking as a result of this scenario? Letting others take the lead? If you are getting the "monkey off your back" is it appropriate or do you need to take responsibility for a different outcome?

Let me repeat … you already have everything you need innately built in you to shape your life your way. It starts with awareness, and knowing you can tap in and turn on the energy surges to move you where you want to go in a positive or negative way. It takes trust, faith, courage, and conviction to build the mindset and rituals to make this happen. Throughout the book I offer tips and suggestions to help you get there.

We can't change others but only how we respond to them. Isn't it great to know that YOU can do this! What you believe makes you who you are!

Here are the four big energy blocks to help you in this process:

- The limited beliefs you hold and the limiting beliefs you accept as true because you learned it from someone else or a situation that happened to you, what you saw in the media, what you heard from authority, what you observed at the movies, etc.

- The false assumptions from the past you bring forth today just because it happened before—it's probably going to happen again. These false assumptions are something you have experienced personally.

- The false interpretations you make—many believe their interpretation is the only possible explanation. Our interpretations represent only one viewpoint among many possibilities available to us. For example, the fear that you are not enough is the inner critic, or what we call a "gremlin," and your "gremlin" is that inner voice that is telling you you're not good enough, worthy enough, smart enough. It urges you to play small and safe. So go ahead and reveal it and name it; this will help to separate it from one's self in order to take back your personal power.

I went through an exercise of creating a hand puppet and gave it a name (as a way of removing it from "I") to say aloud whenever some of those blocks got in my way. My puppet was a sock puppet named Lamb Chop, named after the famous Shari Lewis sock puppet that entertained us on television back in the 1950s and 1960s. So I had a little mini-play with my puppet as a way to detach from emotion and talk through the choices of how it's ME not the "inner critic" that moves me forward in a more positive way.

The Real Cost of Energy

Think about how much negativity is costing you, your family, and the company you may work for. In 2008, Gallup research estimated that negativity costs companies $300 billion a year—and it is safe to assume that number has gone up over time.

How many people do you interact with who are negative, angry, bad for morale, and you wished you didn't have to work with them?

They are known as "energy vampires"—the people that suck the life right out of you—and I only wish I had the tools back then to shift these negative energies. They offer up negative comments such as, "Did I tell you I hate my job and here's why?" or "Can you believe what so and so did in the meeting today?"

Then there are the "dream zappers." "You can't do that!" or "You'll never make a living doing that," or "You should do this instead," and even, "If I were you, I'd do something that you can make real money at."

Then there are the "shrinking violets." "What is wrong with you anyway?" and "Why did I hire you?" or "Can't you do anything right for a change?"

The "demolition team" are the people that get in the way of progress. "We will never make this happen, everyone is clueless here," and "Can't anyone make a good decision for once?"

When I was introduced to the Motivation Factor and Hierarchy of Motivation back in 2009, I was immediately drawn to the simplicity of these processes and the depth of the results that were both immediate and sustainable.

The first level of the Hierarchy of Motivation is about the energy drainers that deplete us throughout the day. Motivation Factor's research shows that 80% of what drains our energy is about people or circumstances that we can't directly influence. Motivation Factor designed a simple and effective way to "unpack" and release these energy drainers and create something you want instead.

Let's use a real situation to demonstrate the ease and shift for this energy drainer situation. It was the Monday of the Boston Marathon; tragedy struck the nation and certainly here in Boston. A few days later the accused bombers landed in my town of Watertown, a shootout took place, one victim died and the other was on the run. We were told not to leave our homes that we were considered to be in lockdown until further notice. My energy drainer was feeling lack of control of the situation and my personal options! This was why:

Four Categories of Energy Drainers

1. *Expectations*—We all have them and when they aren't met judgment happens. Expectations can be about self, others, or a situation. (*I expected to be safe in my home and have the freedom to go about my business.*)

2. *Tolerations*—Annoyances not big enough to change, like the little pebble in your shoe that you don't stop to take out until it hurts! (*Watching non-stop news coverage, and the constant buildup of fear among the residents.*)

3. *Boundaries*—When someone has crossed the line with a side dish of anger. (*I was frustrated that my freedom was removed temporarily, I was feeling unsafe in my own home, and unable to go away for the weekend.*)

CHAPTER TWO: AWARENESS

4. Should-Could-Would—This is our guilt center. We think "I shoulda" all day long—wasting valuable energy. (*I should have left town as soon as I heard the news.*)

Here's another simple exercise to remove energy drainers and create what you want instead. Let me briefly take you through the process using my recent energy drainer experience above.

On a piece of paper I wrote across the top, "Feeling Disempowered Today." I drew a line vertically through the middle and one horizontally through the middle of the page and labeled each box: E for expectation, T for toleration, SCW for should, could, or would, and B for boundaries. I then filled in the boxes with my feelings around disempowerment (listed below.)

Expectations: I expect to be safe, to go when and where I want to go, freedom, and power of choice.

Tolerations: I am tolerating watching the nonstop news, listening to the drama unfolding around us, that one person could cripple a place like Boston for an entire day.

Shoulds/Woulds/Coulds: I should turn off the TV, I could go do some work, I would go to the gym if I could but I can't; I should be grateful that such an effort to catch this guy is a mission for all law enforcement.

Boundaries: My freedom, I feel like a hostage, out of my control and lack of personal power.

What this allowed me to do was vent on paper, release the pent up negative energy, and have the ability to shift it to a more positive level.

I turned the paper over and wrote across the top what I wanted instead: "I want the Freedom to go to Cape Cod."

I drew a line down the middle and on the left side wrote "options" and right side wrote "actions." I created all types of options, realistic or otherwise; after all they are options! I included things like *pack my bags and just go, wait until they catch him and then go, be patient and trust it will work out fine,* and *figure out a plan to get out of town safely and quickly.*

The action I chose was to take the calculated risk of getting out of town by using the back roads away from all the action. I had to take action and that was to pack, check all the windows and doors, let others in my family know I was leaving, and check in along the way to ensure my safety.

It was so eerie on one level, yet daring to take action on the other. The decision was the right decision since as soon as I left the area, I felt relief and safety come back into my life. It felt good to insert my personal power and create choice in my life.

Tip: If you feel stuck, dig a little deeper and add more. Review and see if you make a connection with how much one issue affects all categories. Now ask yourself, "What would I want instead?" Then, create what you want with options/actions moving one of the options to completion. As you work on your own exercise keep in mind you will feel stuck, and this is a great opportunity to work at a deeper level and get resolve, or change what is not working for you.

Personal Needs

Everything that irritates us about others can lead
us to an understanding of ourselves.
—C.G. Jung, Swiss psychologist

What's the difference between values and needs?

Abraham Maslow's hierarchy of needs, developed back in the 1940s, is considered to be the model of psychological motivation of human needs. The five levels of needs include physiological, safety/security, love/belonging, esteem, and self-actualization. The first three levels, what he called "deficiency needs," are basic and at the core for all human beings. We are driven and motivated to always satisfy these needs and if we do not it can cause anxiety, stress, and frustration—making it difficult to move into action. In other words—keeping us stuck. These basic emotional needs that we all have include safety, security, belonging, and certainty.

According to Maslow, the top two levels—esteem and self-actualization—were our "growth levels" that emphasize the human potential and desire for growth. He stated that each level of need must be fulfilled before progressing to the next levels, and indicated that the need for self-actualization would never be completely satisfied. But, in 1970, he revised his theory about self-actualization to be a cognitive need that is a personal motivator for growth and expansion.

This is considered the foundation of all human potential, yet as we evolve as a society so does the deeper understanding of how motivation helps us achieve personal needs, wants, and goals and meaning in our lives.

By now you know that I always have been seeking new knowledge, wisdom, and insight into human potential; when I went through the Motivation Factor certification process I got to experience firsthand the power of applying this assessment to my life and the simplicity in which I was able to move into many "aha" moments.

I covered "energy drainers," which is the first level of the hierarchy of motivation; the second level is personal needs. (This system is aligned with Maslow, yet it is different, and here I will share some of the process with you.)

Personal needs are what motivate our behavior, good, bad, or indifferent, and our personal needs can change over time depending on our situation and what is currently happening in our lives. *Needs* are something thought to be necessary or essentially required to sustain life. Interestingly enough, when I was going through the hierarchy of motivation process I was not consciously aware of my needs, and I was unclear of the differences between values and needs until I worked through this process for a while and discovered what was core and unwavering (values) and what was situational.

Our needs have a stronger pull on us because of the demand to immediately satisfy these needs. The next level is values—the principles we naturally build our life around. For example, when I went through the Motivation Factor process there was an online assessment I took that gave me my top five needs. At the time they were:

1. be heard (the need to be heard and acknowledged)
2. respect (the need to be respected and to be respectful of others)
3. honesty (the need for transparency, truth, and candor)
4. personal power (the need to exercise my personal power and beliefs)
5. balance (the need to take control of my schedule and time, i.e. freedom of choice)

That was totally what I was experiencing in my life, and "to be heard" was number one because at that time, I had no voice! So everything I did consciously or unconsciously was driven by those needs. Before I took the assessment, I was asked to list the five things I disliked about others, and lo and behold the things I disliked most were in total conflict with my immediate needs. I disliked people who talked over me—it was my number one, and as you can see it triggered the top four of my personal needs.

Awareness of our personal needs is a powerful tool since we are constantly confronted with things or people that "threaten" our needs. In Chapter Two, and here, we talk about the brain and how it is comprised of three layers: The reactive brain or reptilian

CHAPTER TWO: AWARENESS

brain (sensory), the social brain (limbic, amygdala, emotive), and the thinking brain (cortex, neo-cortex, hippocampus). The brain uses its own hierarchy for processing.

Here's a scenario as an example of the brain function. You're traveling on a busy highway and your reactive brain is always looking out for either harm or safety. A car decides to pass on the right-hand side of the road and instantly the amygdala flashes an alert message and begins to scan your long-term memory for similarities. You see the car and instead of swerving out of the way, you glance over and decide that if you stay in your lane, the car will pass you with ease.

The amygdala is the control room that takes over the brain in an emergency until the situation is safe again. During this "hijacking of the brain," it releases cortisol, but the hippocampus sees possibilities and finds a solution such as: *Don't panic, stay in your lane, and continue driving safely.*

We know the brain is flexible with the ability to rewire and develop new circuits, and that we can train our brain to create more neural pathways by learning to understand our emotional patterns and what triggers our emotional responses.

As part of this development process I realized naming my needs in my own words meant more awareness for what was important for me and the understanding that everyone is always operating from their own personal needs at all times. It is so powerful to know that when we are triggered by others—it is not them doing something to us—it is them filling a personal need. When a few of us were going through the launch of this program we had many opportunities to test the program, theory, and real-life drama as it was unfolding AND to put what we learned into practice.

One scenario included a dialog between the team members about who would be the right target audience for Motivation Factor, the benefits of this program, and what we would bring to the table. One participant in the discussion was the founder, one was a master at training and development, and one person was the connector and relationship person. It was "lab work" in real time. We had three very different sets of needs that were triggered, challenged, and tested during the discussion. Here is an example of the top three "needs" of each person and how they played out in the meeting:

One person had the need "to be loved, to practice dutifulness, and present personal power," and her actions were to be very supportive and helpful and seek approval along the way—satisfying the need to be loved (belonging), yet she also had a strong desire to exert her opinion, convictions, and power to be heard.

Another person had the need "to be right, experience recognition, and maintain freedom," and her actions were to express with absolute certainty her views—expressed and expected—acknowledgment for her brilliance, and the freedom to participate or not at the level she chose.

And the third person in the room (me) had the need "to be heard, express honesty, and exercise personal power," and I wanted to ensure my opinion and thoughts were expressed candidly, that they were heard and acknowledged, and that my personal power of knowledge, insight, clarity, and conviction was shared with the group.

The conversations were dynamic and creatively demonstrated and—most importantly—a truly empowering way to see how our needs were triggered in real time. We had the ability to work through the issues using the very tools we were about to bring to the market. It was a great case study to use as part of our "launch" presentations.

Our needs can change depending on current situations, yet I would say that the core "needs" for me have been consistent for a long time. Here's where I was confused regarding the difference between values and needs: Respect and honesty are core needs and values too! So are they the same, or different … or both. Needs are filled and values are fulfilled. Values guide a person's needs, wants, and decisions.

And a need can change, where values can evolve at a deeper level. I remember after my throat surgery—over that next year—having

CHAPTER TWO: AWARENESS

a new sense of freedom with a voice that could be heard. I decided to take the Motivation Factor assessment again to see if anything changed, and it did only slightly. My new list consisted of personal power, honesty, respect, to be heard, and freedom. The shift from balance (always weighing things out) to freedom (ability to move with intention) struck me, and upon reflection I would say that I then had my "voice"; it created the freedom to be heard in an open and honest way and exercise my personal power by taking action. There is no real separation between needs, wants, desires, principles, values, and goals; yet each of them play a different role in how we think, feel, believe, and act in creating our A-Game.

Throughout this book you will see those links and connections that we integrate throughout our life working in real time—some at the conscious level and much of the time at the unconscious level.

TIP: My challenge to you is to try to be more in the present moment and to take the time to be aware of what is happening to you, within you, and around you! Consider your needs, values, and wants, and how they might be playing out on your stage of life. What is it you dislike most about the person or situation? Ask yourself what might be a personal need that is triggered at that moment. What steps can you take to eliminate taking it too personally? How can you put yourself in their shoes for a moment and see things differently? Since it is not about you, this is a great way to be detached yet involved.

Values

If you don't stand for something, you will fall for anything.
—Alexander Hamilton, American politician

We all have them, but do we know what they are and how they affect our lives?

A *value* is a belief, a mission, or a philosophy that is meaningful to you. Whether we are consciously aware of them or not, everyone has a set of personal values. Values consist of principles, qualities, or entities that are intrinsically desirable. Values are something we really want and move toward—or something we want to avoid. They are our primary source of motivation.

Personal values guide and propel us to be the best we can be. I remember back when Tom Peters, author of *In Search of Excellence*, focused on why it was important that organizations build their companies to be mission-driven-based with their core values and principles. This is not an easy process to hone in on in regards to the one to ten core values that will appeal to the customer, the employee, and society at large. It was a transition for companies to put a stake in the ground and own their values, and make them public for all to see.

Values have a major influence on a person's behavior and attitude and serve as broad guidelines in all situations. The company I was working for at the time created a new set of five corporate values and released them internally and externally to employees, customers, partners, and stakeholders. They included customer focus, valuing our people, passion for winning, innovation, and working without boundaries. I have to say, there was a lot of confusion, questions, and concerns internally that these were just words on paper—and that they were likely to change with any new leader.

Everyone was good with customer focus, passion for winning, and innovation, and could embrace these no matter who was leading the organization. But people were uncertain about "valuing our people," and what that really meant; and "working without boundaries," which at the time was far more talk than action—where there were many limitations for employees to get things done.

Even though there was a consistent set of values on paper, they did not necessarily align with what was being said or demonstrated

CHAPTER TWO: AWARENESS

based on the behavior and attitude being displayed in the leadership circle. The difference between the "talk" and the "walk" created a difficult work environment at times.

As the core values shifted based on the C-Suite beliefs, there continued to be a departure by employees and customers confused by the mixed messages. The organization lost the trust of people, and ultimately lost its value in the market. It took several years of changes in direction, leadership, and values for it to ultimately cause the company to sell off or close up several of pieces of the business. Clearly when you lose your guiding principles, whether for an individual or a corporation, it can spell disaster.

I was one of the people that struggled with the values the leadership of this company operated under. I was okay with the words and defined my own meaning for them, yet I was in conflict with the behavior demonstrated that was not aligned with my core values. Even though I was there for a very long time, and navigated the waters of change for sixteen years, it only worked out for me because no matter what was happening, I honored my core values in the face of adversity and did not stoop to their level. How did I do this? I reframed the situation so it worked for me. I only represented products and offerings that I could stand behind personally, and I never pushed a client or an employee to disregard their "gut feeling" or questioning of a situation. I was honest with myself and others, was transparent where it was appropriate, and authentically me at all times. Of course, there were struggles between my values, my role, and my obligations to the company and to my customers. Challenges create opportunity, and these were growth moments for me.

Our personal values are ingrained in the fibers of our being. They energize us when we are aligned with them, and consciously or unconsciously, we are seeking people, places, and things that foster the connection to our personal values. We make every effort to form new opportunities, new sources, and experiences to tap into our values.

Several years ago I was at a personal development seminar when the topic of values came up, and we were asked to name our values, what they meant, and why they were important to us. To demonstrate the exercise we were about to do, the trainer asked someone to volunteer up in the front of the room.

A woman named Mary went up on the stage, sat in a high-back chair, and rattled off her list of values, and then the trainer encouraged her to go deeper and add more to the list. What happened was very interesting. The first ten or so were easy to rattle off, and they included things like: job, money, friends, traveling, nice clothes, freedom, and exercise. As he pushed her to go deeper, she became more reflective and emotional when she named love, trust, respect, relationships, safety, honesty, and a few others.

The next step of the list of twenty or so was to pick the top ten on the list. When she completed that, he asked her to then pick the top five! This was more challenging, because all of them seemed important. When she narrowed them to five he asked her to prioritize them. She couldn't do it easily, and he assisted by asking her, "Is honesty more important than love?"

"No," she answered.

"Is respect more important than love?"

"No," and it went on until she was able to prioritize her top five. These were her core values that she operated from—consciously or unconsciously. Her thoughts, behaviors, and actions were driven by her core values.

We don't know what we don't know until we know it, and Mary clearly was able to see how some of the situations in her life that either worked or did not work were directly related to her core values. When they did not work, she was in conflict with a core value.

We were asked to pair off and do this exercise. It was powerful for me to experience, and more importantly, to actually know what was at the core of my actions. What I liked about this process was we used words such as *love* and gave it meaning in our terms. Our meanings of the words were the power behind the conviction of our values.

CHAPTER TWO: AWARENESS

I started to notice how my personal values were driving all my decisions. And it was even more interesting to have made a decision that conflicted with a value, and the outcome was never good, yet it did provide an opportunity to reflect and choose differently in the future for a better outcome.

According to sociologist Morris Massey, there are four major periods a person will go through during the creation of values and personality.

Basic programming occurs between birth and four years old. It's the period when one soaks up everything without filters (not having the ability to determine between useful and un-useful information.)

The *imprint period* occurs from birth to seven years old. We continue to soak up information and pick up and store everything that goes on in our environment from parents, people, and events.

The *modeling period* occurs from age eight to thirteen. We begin to consciously and unconsciously model basic behaviors of other people and may also mimic the values of those people.

The *socializing period* occurs between age fourteen and twenty-one. Young people pick up relationship and social values, most of which will be used throughout life. By the age of twenty-one, the core values are just about complete and will not change unless a significant emotional event occurs or one chooses to evolve and develop values differently.

We do add values to the list, and we often seek new values that are going to move us in the direction of more fulfillment and success. That said, the core values remain steadfast in our decisions—good, bad, or indifferent.

Knowing this to be the case, I just wanted to learn more about how values and needs drive our behavior. (I covered this in the previous section of the book entitled "Personal Needs.")

I was able to group values under a key word, or an umbrella word, to incorporate several similar values that were linked and locked together. Some of those words included respect, honesty, abundance, resourcefulness, love, relationship, courage, and resilience.

Here is the result of the exercise that still holds true to this day.

Integrity, meaning truth, trust, honor, honesty, virtue, ethics, and respect.

Love, meaning connection, partnership, family, intimacy, adaptability, and unity.

Transformation, meaning growth, experience, courage, resilience, self-development, and sharing.

Wealth, meaning abundance, prosperity, resourcefulness, and confidence.

Presence, meaning awareness, adaptability, clarity, curiousity, discovery, and in the moment.

This is what drives all of my decisions, period! When I come across an opportunity that sounds perfect and I get a ping in my stomach, it causes me to push the pause button so I can go deeper, reflect on what I know or don't know, and gather what I need before I make a decision. This is my intuition or inner voice that acts as a GPS for me.

Often it is immediate, and I know the opportunity does not align—or would be in conflict—with core values and principles I have set for myself. And at times that I ignore my inner GPS the feelings of regret and becoming reflective follow.

Speaking of principles, they are equally as powerful at shaping our decisions and our actions.

CHAPTER TWO: AWARENESS

Principles

What you do speaks so loudly that I cannot hear what you say.
—Ralph Waldo Emerson, author

What is a *principle*? It is a fundamental truth or proposition that serves as the foundation for a system of beliefs or for a chain of reasoning. A rule or belief governing one's personal behavior!

I realized at a very young age that I was a very principled person. If someone was being disrespectful, I would call it out. If someone was lying, I had little to no tolerance for them. If someone was cheating, I disassociated with them immediately. Many times it was immediate and definite—no second-guessing. At other times I disregarded what was happening and pushed through the adversity because I felt strongly about something—to ultimately come to the same original decision I disregarded earlier. Oh, what a waste of time! No, it was a great learning experience and without these events in our lives, we would not grow and expand our wisdom, knowledge, and insight.

When you allow something to go against a value, principle, or core belief (however you wish to express it), it does not feel good, it does not serve you, and it devalues you and your beliefs—releasing your power to something or someone else.

My mother use to get mad at me when I stood on my principles; she had no idea or knowledge of how important and core they were to me. She did not have the same set of personal values and did not "get" why it affected me so. She would say to me, "Pride (her definition of principles) is only a five-letter word, and you should stick it in your pocket from time to time." Meaning—let it go!

To this day, I still have the same visceral reaction that comes up from deep down that gets me to stop, stand my ground, speak my mind and/or walk away from the situation. It never comes with regret when you honor your conviction.

Here's a recent example on how my core values played out:

The Massachusetts Conference for Women is a huge event held annually—attracting more than 7,000 women for a day of insight, wisdom, and shared knowledge from well-known and powerful women with messages to move us forward in business and in life. They offered speed coaching to interested attendees that wanted to spend time with professional career experts.

For the past several years I volunteered as a coach along with thirty other career coaches and professionals that belonged to a local professional organization. We had the opportunity to connect with many women and make a small, but impactful, difference in their time at the conference.

Last year the conference decided to work with a national coaching organization so they could serve as coaches at all the conferences they held around the country each year. Perfect, I was a certified coach, knew the drill, and the people involved across the board. I could help bridge the gap between the organizations for a smooth transition.

Both local organizations worked in a complementary way, offering members of either group to attend events at member rates, and everyone got along. As we got close to the event date the new list of volunteer coaches were to be announced, and since I was the first to sign up I figured it was a no-brainer that I would be participating in the program. I received an e-mail prior to the event that said, "We see that you have not renewed your membership and in order for you to participate as a volunteer coach this year, you must sign up!"

The original criteria were coaches must be certified, and willing to spend the day at the event as a volunteer on a first-come, first-serve basis. Since they got such a great response, they decided to add, after the fact, that you must be an active, paying member of the organization in order to participate. A few things happened to me! My visceral reaction was surprise, since I actively helped to smooth the waters between all parties. I offered support and guidance in gathering enough volunteers for the event, and I naturally assumed I was one of these coaches without a doubt. Secondly, I

CHAPTER TWO: AWARENESS

was angry because this flew in the face of my core value of integrity. Third, I did not like being told that signing up for membership was a criterion at that phase of the process. This should have been made clear from the beginning. So for me it lacked honesty, respect, and ethics—concepts that triggered both my values and core needs. When I spoke with the president of the organization, I felt that he chose to not take into consideration all of the factors, he was not willing to make any concessions, and he focused more on the need to be a paid member. As a result I lost a lot of respect for him as a professional and a fellow coach.

To be fair, I realize organizations require money to keep going. I also understand there are rules that apply to everyone without exception. You make an exception for one then you have to do it for others. That said, I do take all things into consideration, and if the rule of being a member had been discussed, that would have played into my decision. As the leader of the organization, I would have wanted to make things right for a person that stepped up to assist without expectations. I would have appreciated the knowledge, expertise, and relationships already established and leveraged them for a win/win/win outcome. This was honoring my core value of integrity.

Another example of core values is: a fellow coach and friend called me one day to ask if he could talk about a personal dilemma he was facing, and feeling conflicted about regarding a decision he had to make quickly.

As certified coaches, there are guiding principles that we all follow and honor as we do our work in the world, and we have an organization that supports coaches and has monthly meetings and events. This particular event was an award ceremony for the "best coach of the year," and his name was submitted on the ballot.

Okay, these award ceremonies happen all the time, what was the big deal? For him, it was going against his core values. He did not believe coaches should be awarded for what they do. He was in conflict with the campaigning for the award versus allowing the award to be given to a deserving person. The popularity contest was a struggle for him. His inner conflict was with his value of self-acceptance and his authentic style versus his passion at being a public representative for the coaching profession. After a dialog with himself and others he decided that it would be okay to participate in the process; a choice for him to honor his value of acceptance. It was being supportive of his coaching community and less about "winning" as it was showing up in a bigger way.

After the event, I received an e-mail saying he did not win and he was okay with that. What was not okay was how he was feeling about the whole process internally and externally. Externally, the event was indeed a popularity contest where the winners clearly did campaigning to members and solicited votes, and this bothered him deeply.

The internal dialog was much harsher on him. His words to me were, "I've spent the day in relative quiet to ponder the TRUE core … what I love, what I long for, what offers me meaning. I guess seeing the opposite helps one to do that."

There are two sides to everything, which appear to be opposite, when in fact they are two extremes of the same thing. For example, heat and cold is a varying degree of the same thing, or light and dark are different shades of the same thing. Without the opposite view, we would not see change or differences. There would be no comparison of good or bad, right or wrong. This is the Universal Law of Polarity. Below is a description of the laws that came to me years ago.

As written in *The Kybalion,* circa 1908, "A Study of The Hermetic Principles of Ancient Egypt and Greece," states there are seven Universal Laws or Principles by which everything in the Universe is governed. The Universe exists in perfect harmony by virtue of these laws. Ancient mystical, esoteric, and secret teachings—dating back more than 5,000 years from ancient Egypt to ancient Greece, and to the Vedic tradition of ancient India—all have as their common thread these seven Spiritual Laws of the Universe.

CHAPTER TWO: AWARENESS

Once you understand, apply, and align yourself with these Universal Laws, you will experience transformation in every area of your life beyond that which you have ever dared to imagine.

Your visions will become clear only when you can look into your own heart. Who looks outside, dreams; who looks inside, awakes.
—C.G. Jung, Swiss psychologist

Chapter Three

Authenticity

> *Every human has four endowments: self-awareness, conscience, independent will, and creative imagination. These give us the ultimate human freedom ... the power to choose, to respond, to change.*
> —Stephen Covey, author of
> *The 7 Habits of Highly Effective People*

Who are you and what do you stand for in the world? This chapter will dig in deeper in areas of self-awareness and self-discovery and how to gain clarity for what is true for you. What influences you, and how you influence others. It's the biggest area of building your A-Game and helps you to discover, build, and bring your authentic self to your work and life.

An "Aha" Moment

> *I hear and I forget. I see and I remember.
> I do and I understand.*
> —Chinese Proverb

I am in constant awe when I learn something new or see something that has been right in front of me all the time and never noticed it.

CHAPTER THREE: AUTHENTICITY

Not too long ago a very good friend of mine was out on his own, going through a divorce after many years of marriage, and was beginning his new life. He invited me over for some advice on how to set up his new apartment. The good news is the furniture he bought was very nice and in neutral colors leaving room to add more color where it made sense. When I walked into the bedroom, everything was white! A down comforter, sheets, blankets, white walls, and a light, nearly-white carpet. It felt like a hospital room.

I asked him if he was open to getting a duvet cover for the comforter, and to adding some color to the room. He asked, "What is a duvet cover?" With a brief description and a trip to Bed Bath & Beyond the journey began. We walked over to the bedding section, and so as not to impose my taste on him, I suggested he look at the different options and see what jumped out at him. I watched him diligently glance at everything, walking up and down the aisles, and after ten minutes or so he came to me and said, "Looks like they don't sell them here." Yet right in front of where we were standing there were at least thirty different duvet cover options to choose from! We can't see what we don't know, and he did not know what he was looking for at the time. Once he made the connection, he was able to make the decision on what to buy.

CLARITY

Clarity is the counterbalance of profound thought.
—Luc de Clapiers, French writer

Many people have called me a "People Whisperer" because of my constant state of being present when I engage with others. I use conscious awareness I like to call CLARITY. It actually is an acronym I created when looking at the steps I took when engaging with others—especially at networking or social events. CLARITY:

Curiosity, Listening, Acknowledging, Reframing, Inspiring Action, Transforming Your New Story. Here's how I applied CLARITY in a real life situation.

Most of you have been to a business event and typically are there to make new connections. So how do you stand out from the crowd? Let me take you through a scenario and how applying CLARITY worked out!

At a women's business networking event there were about fifty people all trying to make connections and business leads to expand their new or existing business. A young woman came up to me and said, "Hi, I am Kellie Smith," and she gave me her business card before asking me who I was. I looked at her card and asked her to tell me more about her company.

"Well, I started this company for people who were out of work; and I wanted to help them find work, and it was originally geared toward teenagers, but I wasn't making any money and when the economy went bad I added everyone."

Whew, a long-winded answer to a simple question and it was not clear, concise, or had any brand impact at all! Here's how I apply my **CLARITY** process, which you too can put into practice at any time!

Curiosity: I was curious, I asked, "What made you start your business?"

Listening: I listened for what she was saying or not saying for clues, and what was her business's unique selling proposition.

Acknowledging: I acknowledged what I thought I heard by using the next step:

Reframing: I repeated back what I thought I heard and inserted more positive language and high-impact words that made her original, long-winded message more clear and concise. It maintained her essence but with more clarification.

Inspiring Action: I offered a way to apply a new approach to express the same thing being said, just differently for a positive result.

Transforming: I taught her how to create an "elevator pitch" or text message version (140 characters maximum) of her new business pitch for these events.

Your (new) Story: I encouraged her to share her message that included her unique selling proposition, and how she benefited clients, using more high-impact words. It was a new way of sharing just enough to pique the interest for others to want to hear more what she had to say.

Talking further, I shared with her what tagline I heard: "linked-in for the linked-out"; a resource center for people looking for work and for those who needed to hire skilled people for odd jobs.

I worked with her and had her practice a new introduction for the remainder of the event that went like this: "Hi, I am Kellie and I have launched the 'linked-in for the linked-out' site," and I had her stop right there until the person asked for more information! This was far more engaging, and had impact to advance the conversation. Kellie came up to me at the end of the event to share her new experience and positive results and wanted to know what else she could be doing differently.

As I began to walk away, she asked for my card and I gave it to her. Typically people go to networking events with the mindset of gathering as many business cards as possible, thinking that approach will result in a successful outcome. Think about this before you exchange business cards:

> *How much time does it take to get cards from others?*
> *More importantly, how much time do you spend looking at the card?*
> *Lastly, what do you do with all the cards you got from the event?*

I seldom if ever, offer my card first, since I am coming from a place of curiosity about the other person. If I were to lead with my card, I would be doing all the talking instead of listening and being present and in the moment. We learn far more listening to others than talking to them. I use a process I call WAIT—Why Am I Talking?—to help as a reminder.

Let me offer this suggestion for future events! Attend with the intention of making connections that are valuable and meaningful, and the number of them really is irrelevant. Resist offering your card first unless it absolutely feels like the right thing to do, and definitely not until you know why you want to stay connected and what you are hoping for as a result of the relationship.

Try it! It is a different approach that is far more engaging (being seen differently from others), to purposeful (being heard through your active listening), and not so exhausting (maintaining high energy)—and you will be remembered in a positive way.

When we come from a place of curiosity—whether engaged in a conversation, or roaming the Internet, bookstore, or anything for that matter—this always will open up the channels to awareness and learning something new as a state of being.

So how do you become more interesting by being interested? Remember to apply CLARITY to any situation when you meet someone new:

> C—Come from a place of curiosity even if you think you know what the other person might say, and ask questions.

CHAPTER THREE: AUTHENTICITY

L—Listen to the person speak; hear what they are saying and what they are not saying.

A—Align and acknowledge what you just heard them say.

R—Reframe in a positive way so they can hear what they said differently and more effectively.

I—Inspire action to hear and speak with more positive words.

T—Transform any limited beliefs that no longer serve them.

Y—Your new story, or version, about the subject or situation, said differently and more positively moving forward.

You can apply the same process when you are doing some self-reflection work around a situation, and this version would be:

Be **curious** about the situation or question at hand.

Listen to your thoughts, beliefs, and your limited talk you are saying to yourself.

Pay **attention** to what you are hearing yourself say.

Replay and **reframe** what you heard differently using positive words.

Have **intentional action** to change the outcome.

Take time to **transform** your new belief system.

Share **your new story** with yourself and others.

Self-Awareness

If you don't know where you are going any road will get you there.
 —Lewis Carroll, English author

Self-awareness is the foundation from which we operate consciously, and provides a continuum on this journey of life. It happens to be a core competency for most women and a natural state of being. Self-awareness is a must-have skill that organizations are seeking as part of their talent management strategies for the future.

How does one become self-aware? If you have been around a while, either in the workforce or even in advanced education, you have taken an assessment or two in your life that gives insight into your skills, behaviors, needs, talents, and overall personality type. Standard assessments include Myers Briggs, the DISC Profiler, Strength's Finder, Motivation Factor, and Emotional Intelligence surveys, to name a few. Believe me, over the years I have taken any and all assessments while finding new ways to improve, expand, and grow—always coming from a place of curiosity about human potential and personal development. It was also a validation of what was working and a reminder on how our work is never done!

I was in the job market when I was offered an opportunity to work with a leading publishing/media company that had one of the oldest, most established magazines in the market. I thought, "Great, at least the doors will open more easily with a company that is well-known." It had fallen on very difficult times, both in the market and in the organization, and was in a turnaround situation. I accepted the position!

Known for being one that faced adversity head on, I loved that the environment gave me a chance to create real personal opportunity from where I was sitting. Aware that I was comfortable with being a calculated risk taker and always looking for the stretch assignments (or task that is out of your comfort zone or area of expertise), I found that this position offered all of it and more. I found being in sales created a sense of freedom, and rewards were based on what you produced month over month. For me the risk/reward was far greater in a sales role on commissions instead of a salaried position, and aligned with what motivated me. The role and environment provided a way to learn, develop, and grow in

CHAPTER THREE: AUTHENTICITY

the business world as a savvy sales person who was able to dictate my future versus it being dictated for me. This was a big turning point in my life.

With change came opportunity. As I progressed through the sales challenges and ever-changing course it led me on the fast track from a sales position to sales management position. Here's what was really interesting—I was making far more money than I expected to make or what they expected to pay as a result of me hitting my stretch goals. And, I was one of a handful of women in the business-to-business world of publishing, let alone this male-dominated company.

There was an opportunity to prove that we were as capable as the men. And in some cases far more creative and patient, building strong, lasting relationships in and out of the organization. Equality was a way of life for me, and it was always a passion and purpose to shine a light on it when it was not happening.

I was doing just that, shining the light on what I wanted next and believing that I deserved it based on my track record. Not so fast, honey! Women getting promoted into management or a leadership role, other than in departments like human resources or accounting, had not been happening. I lived 3,000 miles from the home office, I was on the way up the ladder, and I didn't follow the expectations or rules of the boys' club. I was at a derailing moment in my career, and I did not know it, and I definitely didn't see it coming.

Fortunately, I worked for a senior-level guy named Mike who was well-liked and respected, having been a trailblazer himself over the years. When he came on the scene just a few weeks after I started, he was all about change. Since I was the "new" person and **didn't know what I didn't know** (yep, this is a theme in my life—and most peoples' lives), I tried many different and creative ways around driving business results that he resonated with. What I did not know was that he was sending my stuff to the higher-ups in the company as someone to "watch" for future leadership roles. Today, we would call him a sponsor, more so than a mentor, because of his rank, association, affluence, and support behind the scene.

Mike always was watching my back and was very open and candid about his observations and what potential I had to create a long-lasting career in a leadership role. He offered me the opportunity to go away to Greensboro, North Carolina and attend a week-long program at the Center for Creative Leadership, and I graciously accepted.

Prior to attending the program, several people I associated with were asked to participate in the 360 assessment that provided feedback about me from their perspective. It included my boss, direct reports, peers, and other people in the organization.

Talk about **we don't know what we don't know until we know it** ... what a process of self-awareness and self-discovery that created many "aha" moments that week. The program consisted of personal and 360 assessment results, insightful workshops, group exercises, and one-on-one time with the experts to reflect on areas of development.

Seeing the assessment results for the first time at the training, I automatically defaulted to the negative comments first and paid little to no attention to the positive, which, by the way, there were far more of than the negative. After my initial reaction and emotional meltdown I wanted to flee—and this was day one! I was humbled and wanted to blame others for how I was feeling and realized that the only one who could change the outcome(s) was me!

My feedback indicated that I was not a team player and took matters into my own hands without being inclusive of others during the process. *Hmm ... that's not how I see things. I am a "can-do" person and just make it happen.* Yet my "can-do" attitude was received very differently. It was viewed as competitive, selfish, and lacking in respect for others on the team.

Fortunately, I took the opportunity to sit with the information throughout the next several days and reflected on both the positive and negative, and made the conscious decision to accept the constructive critique with an open mind and open heart.

CHAPTER THREE: AUTHENTICITY

This was the turning point of my professional development; I committed with intention, attention, and action to build my brand on all levels. I integrated all the feedback, tools, and exercises into my day-to-day awareness of my actions and their outcomes. I committed to become an avid student of self and development opportunities. When I returned to the office I contacted all of the people who provided feedback and arranged to have one-on-one, follow-up meetings to share what I had learned. I also asked a few of them to help mentor me in areas where I needed development, and they all said yes!

I found asking for feedback was showing my vulnerability, which I hid from everyone. Yet when I received it and shared it, I was able to build more confidence and trust in myself and others around me.

If you have not actively participated in a 360 assessment, I would encourage you to do so … it is a very illuminating process. And, you might be surprised the difference between how others see you and how you see yourself. There are several companies that offer their version of a 360 assessment as well as many web-based tools you can find online. Here are a few that I have used in the past.

Center for Creative Leadership Assessment

www.ccl.org/Leadership/assessments/assessment360.aspx

Myers Briggs Foundation (MBTI Assessments)

www.myersbriggs.org

The Disc Profiler

www.thediscpersonalitytest.com

Another way I used the assessment process throughout my career was to ask for feedback with a small group of trusted associates and friends that would be willing to be open, honest, and to help mentor me through the areas in which I needed development.

When it comes to assessments we don't have the choice of who we asked to participate—especially if it is company driven. That said; look for allies in the company that can be part of your "entourage," something we will discuss more in-depth in this chapter.

TIP: For this exercise think of the people either in your organization, industry, or community that can serve as the board of directors of "You, Inc." These are people that will challenge, support, and connect you where you need to go and you will be doing the same for them. Plan a strategy to make connections and begin to build your "entourage."

Self-Discovery

In the middle of difficulty lies opportunity.
—Albert Einstein, physicist

Since September 11, 2001, when life as I knew it changed forever, I asked myself a series of questions not once, but often in the days, weeks, and months that followed that awful day. *Why do bad things happen to good people? If life as we know it can change without our consent ... how do we make the life we have matter? What is missing? What do I need to eliminate in order to make room for the things that matter most? What can I do today that empowers me versus disempowers me like the event of that day?*

I found myself keenly alert and aware of everything surrounding my life. I learned later through my brain research that the amygdala

CHAPTER THREE: AUTHENTICITY

always is scanning for a threat. What I also learned was that if the amygdala is over-stimulated while a person is in fight, flight, or freeze mode, it gets frail around the edges—keeping us in a state of alertness even when there is no threat. In this state, one is always on edge and unable to make rational decisions until they can calm down. See more on this topic in Chapter Two.

Being open, curious, present, and in the moment, I always looked for something new and insightful to help me navigate this new way of living, and my safe haven was the bookstore. It was a place that was open to exploration, and since **I didn't know what I didn't know**, I set an intention to be shown what I need to see when I entered into the store. An intention is something that you decide is exactly what you want to happen using affirmative language such as, "I am ready to receive the right books that support me on this journey." Take what you want a step further and add attention to it. To use the bookstore example, first shift your mindset when you enter the store. Be open and present and notice what is coming your way. Next, there is action … the steps you take to notice and decide what you want to do with the information or book you receive. It's always about choice. When I went into bookstores and I picked up a book that did not resonate, I put it back because there always was going to be one that spoke to me—even if it took longer than I expected. This technique was successful not once or twice, but every time.

I always headed for the self-help area and scanned the books—waiting to see what jumped out at me. Those days following 9/11, coupled with the news that my then-husband was leaving, I found myself at a loss and with no real direction. One particular day, the book *The Alchemist* jumped off the shelf. I picked it up and turned to the back cover, and read about how the main character, Santiago, discovered treasures along the journey of personal awareness, knowledge, and essential wisdom. These involved listening to his heart as he learned to read the signs along his life's path, and above all, to follow his dreams. It was the perfect message I needed for that moment.

I so resonated with Paulo Coelho's story on so many levels. First, since I was a little girl, my heart was not just something that pumped blood to keep me alive; it was a focus of intuition and guidance. When fear crept into my life, I would just remember how lucky I was to still be alive to experience this and would ask myself, "How bad could it be, really?" The heart always provides me the wisdom, and my experience is a continuing motivation to follow my dreams and create a life that matters.

Secondly, I so resonated with how **awareness precedes action every time**, and it was a real turning point moment for me to know that I would become the change I wanted to see for my life.

And most importantly, I so connected with the lesson of how to listen and trust intuition, or essential wisdom, which will always guide me where I need to go.

After reading this book, I wanted to learn everything I could about personal power, passion, and possibilities for my self-discovery, and to help others tap into their innate wisdom.

It's the Moments That Matter!

Life is not measured by the number of breaths we take but by the moments that take our breath away.
—Vicki Corona, author

"Right," you say. Here's the deal, and it's true! Let me begin by asking you this ... do you think in terms of moments? Or do you think in terms of events, deadlines, obligations, and other people's needs or requirements? If so, then I would suggest you are not aware or conscious of the moments in your life. There are 86,400 seconds in each day; think of them as being deposited into your human bank account for you to use or lose—they can't be stored or saved for a later date. Or consider if you were given $86,400 each and every day, how would you invest them?

CHAPTER THREE: AUTHENTICITY

Back in 2002, I was feeling stuck and anxious about the future and I was surrounded by all of the negative and fear-based thoughts around my divorce, work, and what the future was going to look like. So, I totally immersed myself in the personal development and self-help world.

I remember hearing about a program in the Berkshires on the East Coast to take place in January (what was I thinking) named "Happiness Is a Choice." It was a week-long program in a rustic environment where you joined a group of thirty-five or so people, all there learning something about themselves. I didn't know what to expect, yet I felt drawn to the program; and it was highly recommended by a friend, so I said yes!

When we started to do all of the "self" work, I was not very comfortable, and was guarded, giving answers off the top of my head … showing no real commitment on day one. I got called out in front of the group by the person leading the program, who asked me why I was there! If I wanted to be there, I had to make a commitment right then that I would be open, willing, and available to do the deep work. Let me say this … I was mad and wanted to "flee" (yes there is a pattern here too). Yet being a stubborn, win-at-all-costs-minded person, I made the commitment to drop my barriers of protection, be okay with vulnerability, and take advantage of the support in the room as I went through this discovery period.

We did a lot of sharing and journaling and over the next few days—it was safe to share openly on most everything. This was definitely new for me and I remained more reserved than the others. There was an opportunity to have a one-on-one session with one of the experts to have a deeper, more intimate discussion about what I wanted in life. She began the conversation with *happiness is a choice* … "what will make you happy is the question?" I said that after this week's experience I wanted to try and make my marriage work and began to cry. She asked me why I was crying and I said because I was happy with the decision. She asked again with doubt, and it hit me right then and there—I had been convincing myself and others that I wanted my marriage to work, but deep down I really wanted a divorce. A new awareness emerged.

Living an authentic life takes work because we have been conditioned by our environment and associations all of our life. Again, the moments when **we don't know what we don't know until we know it!**

Another turning point was when I discovered that my word was so important and honorable to me that there was no way I would not meet and likely exceed what I committed to do. This played out in every facet of my life. Yet recently I was challenged on the very subject by my friend and personal coach on what I was *not* making a commitment to and why!

I had been talking about writing this book for quite some time, and we would get on the phone and discuss the progress. Much of the time I was not happy with myself, the progress, or the results and used lots of excuses as to why I was not further along.

My coach put up with this for a little while as to not take anything away from the creativity of pulling this together. And during a recent coaching dialog she hit me with the question: *Do you feel you have made a commitment to writing this book?* My first immediate answer was "yes," and then the thought hit me like a two-by-four … had I made a real commitment or was it just a desire? As we delved deeper into the discussion I realized that I did not consciously commit to the project for fear of failure or not meeting the commitment. When I stayed in a vague place, I could work at my pace and maybe get it done. Yet, if I made the commitment, there was no question that it would get done. "So what is the problem?" she asked.

Then the inner critic raised her voice and said, "Maybe I am not smart enough to do this … and who wants to hear what I have to say? This type of book already has been done before, what more could I add?" These inner-critic messages kept me from putting a stake in the ground and committing to bring this book forward.

CHAPTER THREE: AUTHENTICITY

As a result of making a verbal and written commitment to myself and my coach, the book began to emerge with more energy and determination than just talking about it. Commitment is more than a word—it aligns with my personal values of integrity, honesty, and authenticity, and moves me into action and toward positive results.

Law of Attraction

> *Cherish your vision and your dreams as they are the children of your soul, the blueprints of your ultimate achievements.*
> —Napoleon Hill, American author

I have read hundreds of books and attended several live events from the personal development gurus. I would say that I was attracted and addicted to the learning opportunities that opened me up to the unlimited possibilities I could create in my life.

I was so inspired by what I was discovering, trying, and embracing as a new way of life, and the results were continually validating these unlimited possibilities. It was this validation that taught me "what we think about comes about," and I put this to the test every chance I could.

Have you heard about the Law of Attraction? It was a central part of both the book and the movie version of *The Secret*. It was a huge game changer back in late 2005-2006 for those seeking meaningful change and creating their desired life. I already had been exposed to many of the teachings from the movie, and confirmed my belief that this principle really works when I created my first vision board. It was a Sunday afternoon in June of 2005 when I poured myself a glass of wine and began going through all of the magazines I had, looking for things of interest. They included open-spaced and unique houses in the hills; a beautiful resort in Mexico; lush, green, landscaped yards; and splashes of color that resonated with me. In addition, I cut out pictures of romantic places with couples sharing the moment; Capri, Italy; a golf course; and a few good-looking golfers; and the then current Mayor Newsom of San Francisco, who was extremely handsome, smart, and making a difference in the city. I wanted to meet him! I wanted to play more golf! I wanted more color in my life, and I had a strong desire to travel.

And I wanted to figure out an exit strategy from my current company, and start over with my own company for many reasons I will cover later in the book.

So what happened almost immediately after randomly cutting out all of the pictures? I got a call from a friend to play golf that week and an invitation to meet the mayor at a private fundraiser event that week. I met an interior decorator at a restaurant that offered to help me with colors for my townhome. Everything in the pictures started to appear … coincidence? Hmm, I don't think so.

It got better. The following week I found an advertisement for a free seminar on the Law of Attraction and wanted to go. Obstacles got in the way of me making it in time so I said, "Forget it, I can't get there," and then suddenly everything cleared in order for me to go!

I walked in late, sat near the door for an easy exit in case it wasn't resonating with me, and what happened next was amazing! Not only did it resonate, it was screaming at me … "Go to this program!" I had just transferred the exact amount of money needed for the trip into my bank account; and it was in Capri, Italy! Another synchronicity occurred when I arrived at the hotel—the balcony and view from the hotel was the exact picture I had on my vision board!

This process continues to work today. I would encourage you to consider creating a small vision board and experiment with it. Here are a few ideas on how to get started:

- Collect all the magazines you have access to and with no agenda, flip through the pages and tear out whatever catches your attention—don't overthink and keep moving. It could be pictures,

CHAPTER THREE: AUTHENTICITY

words, recipes, or anything that resonates with a desire you might have.

- There are several options on how to display them, and the point is to display them where you can see them in sight every day. This helps reinforce the vision and desire you want to attract into your life.

- You can have a personal vision board and a professional vision board. Once you have achieved any of the items on the boards, replace them with something new so you always are manifesting what you want.

There is another version of the vision board you can carry in your purse. Write down at least 100 things you want to do in your life. They don't have to be significant, just meaningful to you. It may be difficult to come up with a list of 100; stretch to a number that is most comfortable for you. I set out to create this list while I was in Italy. I typed it up and kept it with me at all times. Whenever I experienced something on the list—I would cross it off or add to it when applicable.

This was very empowering and inspiring for me as I walked my journey. The most exciting part of the process was seeing the results at all levels. **What we think about comes about.** My list was complete within three years, and I just created a new list this past year.

Some examples of what was on my list included: traveling to Italy, visiting a resort in Mexico, having a massage monthly, eating in one new restaurant a month, or having a house on the Cape or in the mountains, and enjoying romantic dinners and good conversations. Simple, right? Yet I find that we are most often on autopilot—we are just letting time run us instead of actively applying intention, attention, and action toward the things that bring us joy! Take time to celebrate your life by giving yourself the small pleasures that make you happy.

Influence

Think twice before you speak, because the words and influence will plant the seed of either success or failure in the minds of another.
—Napoleon Hill, American author

Influence is the ability to change or shift, and affect or alter, the events or outcomes through direct or indirect action. Influence is a combination of skills: communication, negotiation, self-control, integrity, organizational awareness, and personal power. It is the ability to change other's perceptions, while maintaining balance in one's own integrity and values. Influence is core to everything we choose to do or not to do.

Influence is a big category that has many labels that are distasteful to many women such as: political, sales, manipulation, game players, con men ... and the list goes on. What we are going to explore in this chapter is the power of influence, and what happens when you develop and apply these skills. We also will look at the dark side of not being authentically "savvy" and the limitations we set for ourselves.

What I value so much is to have experienced many things in my career that I could not name or even understand until much later in life. When I left my corporate life I then was able to see all of the obstacle courses I had endured and the skills and gifts I received as a result of the experiences.

Most of my entire work life was in sales, sales management, and executive leadership roles that required "influencing" others around some form of action and outcome. I was helping others to see the benefits of seeing things differently.

I believed in what I was saying or asking. I absolutely felt authentic and real, and if it was not the case, I either had to find a way to reframe and deal with the situation so it was manageable for me, or I opted not to move forward until it felt right and aligned with my core values. Our core values are running in the background at

CHAPTER THREE: AUTHENTICITY

the unconscious level until something is triggered and brings us into conscious awareness requiring action. An example of this is about my core value of integrity. My integrity is not something I think about—it just is! If I was asked to go back to a client after they said no to an offer numerous times and instead offered them an exclusive if they bought right then … at a deeper discount for signing up first, my reaction was *Absolutely not!* This would not be fair to all of the customers, and the opportunity should be made so that everyone had a shot at the deal! Integrity of fairness was at play here.

Let's walk through a scenario that covers many facets of influence. I was offered a huge stretch assignment that would shift the way we went to market in the publishing industry. It was an opportunity to shift from selling a single product to selling a suite of products across the globe with a single point of sales contact.

This was a great strategy for our external customers but a major threat to our internal clients—the other business leaders and sales teams both domestic and international. They perceived these changes would take away their business opportunities, existing customer relationships, and potential revenue. Here is the background on me and the company I was working for. I was a woman working with mostly men (publishers) that were in charge of their domain, relationships, sales teams, revenue targets, P&L (Profit and Loss), and ultimately the results of their business. The international sales team did not report to this division, and they too were being asked to "play nice in the sandbox" for the good of the customer.

The sales team directly reported to their publisher, yet they were being asked to also report to me! This was not going over very well. I would need to tap into and utilize every leadership skill and talent (I will reference this later in the chapter), and I had to develop a consistent approach that would inspire others and get results from the inside out.

Political Savvy

Affluence means influence.
—Jack London, American author

What is the feeling that shows up for you when you hear you need to be more "political?" If you are like many of the women I know, including myself at one time, it is: *I despise politics. It makes me angry and anxious to think I need to be a political person to get by in this job. I can do my job well and work hard and won't have to be political because my job performance will speak for itself!* Or at times "political" feels manipulative and unauthentic—the "icky" feelings that we get when we are not aligned with our core values.

The Center for Creative Leadership has done a tremendous amount of research on all areas of leadership, and specifically on gender-based differences. Here's what it indicates: Women perceive organizations as being more political than men do, and women managers view politics as "evil," and find engaging in political behavior to be difficult and painful.

The research indicates the way men and women are socialized differently plays a role in these perspectives. Men tend to be part of the "insider club" where the rules of the game are made clear early by the other men. Women tend to be "outsiders." The rules women follow are more traditional and part of a belief system that tells them if they work hard enough and have enough expertise, they will get ahead.

Okay, full transparency here … I did feel like an "outsider" at times, but it did not stop me from demonstrating my contributions, nor did I believe that someone would notice what I was doing and get ahead that way. I am going to discuss how to "ask" for what you want because that is the best way to create your desired outcome in work and life. There is more on this topic in the Ask/Negotiation section of this chapter.

CHAPTER THREE: AUTHENTICITY

Political skill is vital for a woman's career advancement; not just to break through the glass ceiling, but the "glass walls" that limit their movement even across organizations.

This is when you hear people saying they are "stuck" or are in roles that have no responsibility for profit and loss. I will discuss further how important it is to be perceived as strategic and knowledgeable about P&L statements in Chapter Five.

We have made progress, yes, but women still are apt to find themselves in situations where opportunities for promotion, access to mentors and sponsors, and encouragement to take risks is absent. These barriers make it more critical to develop and embrace being politically savvy.

During many of the coaching sessions I have had with my clients, the subject of politics and how to get around them was a topic that came up in most engagements. Curious to learn here, I developed a brief questionnaire to share with my network of savvy women leaders and get their point of view. They shared these thoughts:

"Political behavior is self-serving and a way to promote personal and professional gain."

"It's big girl and boy bullying."

"Game-players looking to make themselves look good at the expense of others."

"Backstabbers and low-lifes."

There were several that felt it was a must-learn for fear of losing their jobs or stunting their career opportunities.

Then there are others like myself who have learned being politically savvy can create desired outcomes in a positive and authentic way. Personally, I have developed strong relationships across the board and learned at the "relationship" level what was important to know, who was important to know, and what did they need to know about me to **be seen, be heard, and be remembered**. This, by the way, is an ongoing process for the rest of your life in and out of work. I learned that being politically savvy did not mean "I win, you lose," it was a way for a win/win/win most of the time. Since the word "political" bothered me, I opted to reframe it to the word "influence," which has a better energy around it.

Being a master of reframing something so that it works for me, I wanted to learn as much as I could about how to "influence" as a way of being "politically savvy," and to experience the results needed to move toward action and results. There was the "insider's club" that made so many of the strategic decisions for the rest of us and I wanted to be right there. How was I going to get invited in? Who did I need to know more of and why? What value do I bring to the table and how will it make a positive impact? Knowing the basics of whom, what, and why really helped formulate a strategy to get results. I did get invited to participate on the President's Advisory Council, which consisted of only twelve people across the entire organization. My area was "compensation" and I was able to strategically demonstrate a new and innovative plan to engage employees beyond money. I researched the "best practices" of complementary industries to learn what was working for them and how it shifted engagement in the workforce. It included an ongoing dialog with employees with creative contests, stretch goals, and community involvement inside and outside the company. It was the thought process and delivery that caught the attention of the right people at the right time that helped me leverage future challenges and opportunities. It was another turning point moment and a lever that catapulted my career.

We'll go back to my earlier example of how influence would help me with my new stretch assignment. We were at a point in the marketplace where we needed to step out of the box that our competitors put us in, which was creating a lose/lose/lose situation across the board. It would require making bold and risky strategic changes that would clearly shake up the status quo!

I built a strategic road map on who needed to know and what they needed to know in order to get the buy-in I needed. Once I determined who the players were, I then did my homework on each of them on a personal level (when possible) about their management style and about their best business practices. I included information on what already was working well, what we could emulate in a modified way, and how best to communicate change to all the parties involved.

I asked questions such as: Who else do I need on my side to support the ideas and creative, out-of-the-box strategies that are being suggested? And, who do they know that I could bounce ideas off of before I make the pitch to the players? Part of this process was using the well-known and effective SMART goals along the way to keep the progress going. SMART goals are Specific, Measurable, Attainable, Reasonable, and Timely.

I found opportunities to share interesting business articles or to discuss industry trends that aligned with this group's interests, which gave me the ability to make connections on as many levels as possible. I attended events and networked with every available person that could help me open doors, or better yet, add resources and information to the strategic plan I was proposing.

When I felt prepared, researched, networked, and supported, I made the re-connections with the CEO, president, and CFO, gave the "pitch," and asked for support in bringing it to the market. I got the go-ahead from the highest levels in the organization, and their personal support and interest to see this succeed.

Not only did it succeed, it also was a huge success for my organization, our customer base, and a shake up for the competition to stop resting on their laurels and step up to meet us at our level. It earned me a seat at many new tables in the future.

Authenticity and Influence

Let others see their own greatness when looking in your eyes.
—Mollie Marti, psychologist

If you are politically savvy you are most likely effective in influence and persuasion of others in a sincere, authentic manner. And why does this matter in developing your authentic leadership brand?

Here are at least six key areas of leadership worth noting—as it continually affects how you are seen, heard, and remembered!

- **Networking.** The ability to know where to go, who to seek out, and how to influence your professional connections in a more defined way. We will talk about networking further in this chapter.

- **Social Astuteness.** Knowing your audience and what they have in common with you. Understanding as much about the social circle, what's relevant and timely for these influencers, and having the ability to speak their language. Doing your homework and staying current on news and events in the industry.

- **Interpersonal Influence.** Knowing what your core values are and how the connections you establish align with them! Being open, honest, and trustworthy, and always coming from a place of authenticity. Incorporating your core values into your authenticity.

- **Ability to Get Visibility.** What do you bring to the table that is unique, creative, and memorable? Who can help you get in front of the right audience and why would someone want to do it for you? Develop your professional brand as a stand-out in the crowd—more on this in this chapter.

- **Build Up Your Human Capital.** This includes your wealth of knowledge, wisdom, insight, and skill set that have economic value for the economy as a whole. See Chapter Five for further information.

- **Think Before You Speak.** Think, then pause before you speak, step up, and take action. Having a plan and working your plan. Prepare, prepare, prepare … and then let it go. Knowing you did your homework and trusting you are ready and able to be the best you in the moment. Take the step!

Communication

Words mean more than what you set down on paper. It takes the human voice to infuse them with shades of deeper meaning.
—Maya Angelou, author and poet

As a master "connector," I attend a lot of events every month where there is an opportunity to engage with people I know, want to know, or make a point of knowing when I get there. Here are some prompts to help you prepare for such an event:

- How is your energy level around being at this event? Check in and see how you are feeling. Is it upbeat or are you dreading the ordeal? Either one will shift your energy—you are in control here.

- What are you going to wear and why are you deciding on the outfit? Check in with how the outfit makes you feel. What is the feeling you want when you put that outfit on? If it does anything but lift you confidence—change outfits.

- What is your "story" for those you know and want an update on your life? What have you prepared to say, and why does it matter for others to know? Is it moving you forward or staying in neutral? What do you want people to remember?

- What is the story for those you want to meet? Introductions make or break a new connection. Be thoughtful and practiced about what you want to say. You can have a few different ways of telling your story as long as they are consistent with your professional brand.

- And, what is your memorable, catchy, personal statement to open up for further dialog? Create something that will stick and be remembered easily. Too many words and you lose people's attention or memory capacity. Make it short, sweet, impactful, and remembered.

- What is the feeling you want others to have as a result of connecting with you? Think about it, what are the three words you always want people to say about you? Align with the positive and enthusiastic words that create the energy level you resonate.

A fact to remember: People always gravitate to the strongest energy levels and most often at the unconscious level. If you are a positive person, it will feel good to others and they will gravitate to you. If you are a negative person, people will avoid you. Next time you are at an event, test the reaction of how people connect with you when you are being positive, and again when you are being negative, and observe what you see. Of course only attempt this when the risk is low!

That's the prep work. The real work comes with being open, present, flexible, and in the moment (as much as possible) and engaging from your authentic self no matter what is happening. By doing the prep work, you have consciously mapped out how to **be seen, be heard, and be remembered**. Now let it go, and trust that it will turn out exactly as it is supposed to happen.

Recently I was invited to speak at a women's business networking breakfast event. Prior to attending, I checked out the event, the mission statement of the organization, and the calendar of events to get a sense of the audience. I looked at the recent pictures from past events to get an idea of how people dressed when they attend the event. And, I checked out past speakers to learn what some of the themes were in the past. I discovered a tremendous amount of insight by doing some homework online.

In my head and then on paper, I wrote down my "tagline" and my three follow-up words I wanted people to associate with me. What is a tagline? It is a key phrase that identifies you or your business by capturing the essence of three elements: your mission, your promise, and your brand. When choosing your tagline, be clear, concise, and ask the question, "So what?" People are only interested in how something serves their needs. So choose what helps you prepare your conviction and purpose about what you are doing or saying at that time. Be sure it reflects your image, differentiates you from the competition, and lets your personality show.

I work with Twitter's perimeter of 140 characters to build my tagline. It keeps it tight and tweet-able as well as easy to remember: "I help others discover, build, and bring their A-Game—be seen, be heard, and be remembered." My three key words are: present, curious, and engaging.

TIP: Write all the keywords that describe what you do and work it down to a tweet-size that has impact and influence. Remember when you deliver your tagline always pause so that others ask you to tell them more about you and why you do what you do! Refine, rewrite, and rehearse your tagline until is flows with ease. You can have several versions of the same thing for different audiences or business settings.

So many women tell people who they work for and the job title they have. Let me suggest you repeat your name, what you do, and then the company you work for. *Yes, I am Carole Sacino, and I help to change people's lives working at the Turning Point Institute.* I did not say I was a CEO; if someone asked then I would tell them. No matter if you work for yourself, or a company, your title need not be distinguished before it needs to be. We know that judgment is always happening consciously or unconsciously, and you have the choice to create the impression you want to express.

Let me expand on this ... if we are being our authentic selves this is what will show up. When you are present and in the moment, you are actively listening and engaging in the moment and trusting your authentic self will show up. Being present, in the moment, and flexible allows you to be there to support others and not your personal agenda. This is where knowing who you really are and why you do what you do will reveal itself to others. You've been doing the work on yourself your whole life, and are exactly where you are meant to be now!

Okay, so you are thinking, "Yeah, but ..." and what follows are those limited beliefs that pop up and sabotage all of your confidence and ability to step out and up in the moment. I know, I get them all the time—and by the way, they never go away. And for me that is a good thing, because each time I am challenged it is an opportunity to make a choice on how I want to handle the situation.

Did you know, based on neuroscience of the brain, it takes only ninety seconds for a thought or feeling to go away unless we place meaning and effort to keep it active? We control this! It is a moment of personal power to know we can change our thoughts, feelings, and actions to meet our desired outcome. We cover more about the brain in Chapter Two.

So back to this event I was attending. As I was driving down I got this knot in my stomach about standing in front of seventy-five or so women, talking to them about what I knew. What! And the little voice rose up and said: *Who wants to listen to you ... you're not as smart as you think, you know. And what about your voice ... will they really hear you?* All true! And as this came up for me, I consciously made the choice to enjoy the challenge, and to see the

CHAPTER THREE: AUTHENTICITY

opportunity to be my authentic self no matter what, and to trust I was doing the best I could. I let it go. When I got to the conference it was bustling with conversation, and there was an array of dress styles in the room, so no matter what I was wearing, it would fit in. That was the good news ... the better news was at the end of the day, I dressed for me and what made me feel my most powerful self, and that always works!

We all have a personal style, which is a key component to our personal and professional brand. It adds to how people see, hear, and remember us. For me, I am still most comfortable wearing a jacket either over a dress or pants. I enjoy wearing high-quality clothes and of course good shoes. Both men and women check out shoes and nails. Why do I wear a jacket? Mainly for the pocket to carry cards, pen, money, and to have breath mints at all times!

I did not get a chance to engage prior to the kick-off of the event, nor did anyone even try to engage me. I found that to be odd ... not because I was speaking, but because I was a new face in the room! My observation was that people connected with the people they knew with ease and stayed there! Being a student of observing women in motion, this is what I see at every event by the majority in a room.

I am not a fan of having to stand up and do the ten- to thirty-second introduction to the audience, yet it is a great way to get an idea of who is there and whom you want to make a connection with before the end of the day. As I watched and listened I was struck by the nonverbal communication—also known as our body language—and energy level of each of the women during their introductions. I'll share a few observations I had about the majority—and yes there are always a few exceptions—and these were the standout moments that separated them from the crowd.

As these women stood, there were some of the obvious nonverbal cues: wringing the napkins as they spoke, holding their hands crossed in front of their lower bellies; a few leaned on their chairs as they spoke, many of them shifted from side to side as they spoke. Almost all either looked down or up as they spoke and a few played with their name tag or necklace. And lastly, a few stood with legs crossed so tight I thought they were trying to shrink inward as much as possible.

Wow, what an observation that, for me, was a present, in-the-moment opportunity to address this as part of my talk—I threw out whatever opening I had in mind and went for it. As I was introduced and came to the stage I decided to demonstrate the nonverbal element I observed with the crowd by speaking softly (well, I had mastered that over the years) and looking down, playing with my napkin, and saying "hmm" and "oh" for what seemed liked forever—but it only was for about twenty seconds. I stopped, turned away from the audience and then turned back around into the room as my authentic self with confidence and ease. I then asked them, "Now what did you see, hear, and remember?"

I requested of the audience to shout out what they saw and their feedback were things such as uncertainty, fear, and doubt as to why I was in the front of the room. This was excellent feedback and I thanked them for sharing what behaviors they observed.

I then asked them, "Now what did you hear?" They told me, "passivity," "a lot of 'hmms'" and filler words such as "like" and "you know what I mean." Acknowledging the feedback, I asked if the presentation had stopped when it did, what would they have remembered about me? They told me, "Someone who lacked confidence and was disengaged with the audience," and one person said, "Boring!"

This was a jumping-off point that opened up the discussion around how the limited-belief talk we have with ourselves, and the mind chatter we have going on in our heads, is reflected in how we show up—whether we are talking or not. This provided an opportunity to bring awareness to the importance of our nonverbal cues, and how we are responsible to show up how we want to **be seen, be heard, and be remembered**. We talked about the power of awareness, and changing our behavior—with practice—becomes a natural state of being authentically us.

Then what happened? The microphone was not working! A few years ago I would have totally panicked, and the little girl with doubt, fear, and anxiety would have shown up. It was a huge opportunity for me to own my voice and demonstrate it through my story for other women in the room. It was a live and in-the-moment life lesson of taking a challenge and finding the opportunity for a win/win/win outcome.

For years I had in the back of my mind "fake it until you make it" whenever I was stretching into new areas of my life, especially during my career in the corporate world. It was risky to show failure at any level, and often times it determined how I was measured or judged, how it affected my job security, promotions, and compensation. Showing failure is an internal and external dialog that is happening much of the time. Our internal dialog is what matters most and influences how we show up in the world and how others make decisions. We are in control here!

Even though it was only a saying I used, the words became real and it did produce results. *Act as if and then become* turned out to be true for me. Before a sales call or any important meeting I used to practice being confident, passionate, engaging, and enthusiastic, and of course comfortable in my own skin. That was the "fake it until you make it" muscle I was building over time. When I was in this frame of mind, I believed it to be true and authentic, and sure enough it was and is true today.

"Our bodies change our minds—our minds change our behavior—our behavior changes our outcome." This is a quote from Amy Cuddy's TEDTalks conversation—you can find it on YouTube. If you are not familiar with the TEDTalks series it is worth checking out. They began several years ago featuring speakers with a unique message or story that could impact change for others. The format is held as a live event, and limited to a maximum of seventeen minutes to make the speaker's compelling message stick. Every topic imaginable can be found with the TEDTalks.

When I watched Cuddy's talk it totally validated my lifelong experience of personal power, presence, and possibilities. The power of our nonverbal communication affects how it shapes the way others see us and demonstrates how we see ourselves consciously or unconsciously.

During one of Cuddy's TEDTalk sessions she discusses the shift in hormones such as testosterone (power hormone) and cortisol (stress hormone). She indicates that it's the power pose/position that put us in the higher testosterone levels—which includes assertiveness, confidence, and optimism—and less of the cortisol or stress levels we have. It is the pose we take to either increase or decrease one of these hormones and it affects how we are perceived and to when one goes up the other goes down. Some of these power pose/positions would include a wide-open gesture, relaxed with hands behind the head, standing with both hands leaning on the desk, and both hands on the hips. "Being large and in charge" paints a power position in my head.

Powerless pose/positions are when we wrap ourselves up to be small, cross our arms tightly across our chest, slump in the chair … anything to not get close to another human being.

When we are in a state of stress or threat, our bodies are hardwired to produce either testosterone or cortisol. Ladies, we tend to produce more cortisol that puts us into a "survival" mode, and likely into a powerless position by default. That's not to say we don't have the fight/flight adrenaline rush when we need it, but generally speaking cortisol is more prevalent for women.

Excessive and prolonged stress causes the body to produce too much cortisol, which can play a role in craving comfort food, overeating, feeling fatigued, and storing excess fat.

Words We Use Matter

What we say matters! How we say it matters! The WORDS we use matter! It can and does change your life!

The more I am out there connecting with people through my seminars, workshops, or talks, the more I can sense the need to create more

CHAPTER THREE: AUTHENTICITY

awareness around the power of the words we use and how we use them and how that has a major impact on the results we get.

There is a widely-used, over-simplified statistic in communications pioneered by Professor Albert Mehrabian, author of the book *Silent Messages*, which also has been used in the business world as a reference for effective communication. The formula states that for effective communication when discussing emotions and feelings 55% is made up of body language (how people read you), 38% consists of tonality (how people hear you), and 7% is made up of words (spoken). The 7%-38%-55% rule helps explain how nonverbal and verbal communication work together.

The spoken or written words we use have meaning and energy that affect how people feel what you are saying and how they are ultimately going to relate to the conversation or message. I believe that more focus on the words we use is more critical today than ever before.

Our communication style and modality is quickly changing from face-to-face to everything digital. Think about how you make connections and conversations today. E-mail, text, Facebook, status updates; and who knows what is to come? It is safe to say that words are playing a critical role in what you are saying and how you hope it is being received. Think about how many messages you have received that you interpreted differently than what was intended. Why is that? Because we put our filters on what we see, hear, and remember. Words we use have energy and affect us at the conscious and unconscious level.

The words you send electronically are written based on what your nonverbal communication is at the time of writing it. Press the pause button and take a minute to reflect on how you were feeling when you wrote it before you send it!

Because of the change in how we communicate, I would place more value on words, moving it from 7% to 38% on the importance scale. Tonality is valuable but less so than the written words we use combined with our nonverbal expression.

Most of what we say is not well thought out in advance—especially the thoughts that pop into our heads or the immediate responses to something we know (we are operating at the unconscious level most of the time)—and we go with it. Much of what we think about is limiting, and creates low energy or negative outcomes that get in our way of desired outcomes.

Let's look at a few examples of limited thoughts:

I can't find time on the schedule for myself. I don't have the ability to get it done. I know I won't get that raise. It won't happen. These are all negative outcomes! You can stop them simply by changing your internal self-talk, bringing positive things into your life, and by reframing your statements to:

I AM ... is the statement of who you are. *I am competent and skilled.* **I AM** ...the two most powerful words you can use. I AM affirms positive action taken already.

I CAN ... is the statement of your potential. I can make time on my schedule for me, it's important to me.

I WILL ... is the statement of the positive change in your life. *I will get this raise, I deserve it.*

AND ... is another power word to use. It's not "or," "if," "but" ... it's "and I" ... bringing forward movement, and positive energy. *I am living an abundantly full life AND enjoying it!*

One of my favorite mantras, a constant reminder, is: **What we think about comes about.** Another great one is: "What we focus on grows bigger." Whether positive or negative it will arrive, and it takes the same energy and effort to think about it ... so why not choose a positive word that creates a positive thought for a positive outcome? An example of *what we think* *about comes about* came the other day, when my friend was worried about the aggressive Boston drivers on the highway and how fast they go. "I am afraid of getting into an accident," she said. I immediately share, "What we think about comes about." A little laugh, a hug, and off she went. The very next day she called me to tell me about the terrible accident she was in that night—exactly what she feared.

Another example was when I cut out the picture of Capri, Italy and put it on my vision board, and three months later not only was I in Capri, but I was at the exact place from the picture!

What we think about comes about—one simple phrase can be one of the greatest gifts you give yourself!

TIP: Become mindful of what you are thinking about and how you can reframe your thoughts in a positive way. If you say something that doesn't feel good—pause, reflect, and reframe. It just takes a moment to make the shift, and it's the moments that matter in how our life is created. You are in charge of it, and you can start right now to change the outcome.

Gender Communication: Status-Driven Vs. Connection-Driven

Research shows that many men socialize to view the world through a hierarchical lens and put their attention and energy toward independence and establishing a high-status role with others. Competing for status is their way of connecting with others. Some of the conversational social "rituals" include: oppositional banter, playing devil's advocate (I do this one a lot, hmm …), reporting facts and data points, interrupting, storytelling (this is good for both genders to incorporate), teasing, and one-upmanship.

Women are more interested and motivated by the connection they make with others, maintaining an appearance of sameness and equality, and seeking common ground as a way of inclusiveness. It's all about the relationship! Conversational social "rituals" include: asking questions, listening, complimenting, finding commonalities in experience, complaining about work (trouble talk), sharing secrets, and attending to others' needs—women are the helpers!

Direct and Indirect Communication Styles

Both genders use varying levels of direct and indirect communication based on their cultural and particular differences and their comfort levels. Research suggests that women tend to be more indirect to get action from others where men are more direct in the asking.

Women have been criticized by men as being manipulative (women accuse women of this too) because of the indirect approach, where men can be perceived as bossy or bullies because of their direct approach. When either gender uses a conversational approach, not perceived to fit to its gender labels, it can be a mismatch. For example, when a woman is being bossy or too direct she gets the "B" label. If a man communicates too much empathy or asks too many "feeling" questions it could be perceived as "different," "soft," or "weird."

Women consistently use or overuse rituals that diminish their ability to influence. Some examples of this include:

I am not sure about xxxx however—
I don't know if this will work, but—
You have probably already thought of this, but—
Maybe it's me, but! (*But* can be a killer in conversations.)

Or all the filler, hedges and question tags such as: *um, you know, well, like* (the filler words); *kind of, sort of, something like, maybe* (the hedge words). Have you noticed when someone seems to lack confidence or is nervous and unsure of themselves they use a lot of filler words? Next time you have the opportunity to listen to someone who may be nervous or lacks confidence, see if you can spot the filler words and how often they use them; it's another opportunity to build awareness.

Then there the question tags: That was well written, wasn't it? I believe this is the best way to do it, OK? We seemed to hit the mark, didn't we? All said in up-talk, the rising inflection that adds a questioning tone.

And of course there are the apologies. Women are cited for apologizing often when it is not even their fault. "I'm sorry," is not as much an apology from women, but the language of empathy. Men can misinterpret this.

It is definitely a different style of communication and can change the dynamic of the conversation. Awareness of the words we use or don't use matters.

TIP: Remembering to be present and in the moment with active listening helps us connect to the language and mirror the other person. Take the time to pause and choose what and how you say something. It becomes the way to connect in as your authentic self. **Awareness precedes action every time.**

Beyond Networking

You get the best out of others when you give the best of yourself.
—Harvey Samuel Firestone, business leader

When you ask how many people like to network … maybe a few hands go in the air. During my corporate life, and of course being in sales, we were not only asked to network, it was a regular event. Personally, I love "networking"; and what made this easier for me was reframing the word as "making a connection."

When I first got into sales I found having to attend live events and tradeshows to be daunting and overwhelming; especially not having the ability to talk in loud environments. It was not something I liked at all. This was definitely a time to use reframing of what to expect and what was expected.

Planning

To be effective and efficient at networking, planning is a key factor. If I was attending a major tradeshow I would do as much pre-planning and scheduling as possible. Many of the attendees were there to "sell" and connect with people they wanted to do business with, and when you were on the "sales" side, trying to get vendors to consider something was not always a priority for them. This was when relationships mattered—more on this shortly.

Several weeks before an event, I would send invitations for coffee or lunch meetings. If not successful there, I would schedule a time on the tradeshow floor to meet (this rarely worked out), and if not successful with connecting before the show, I did have the show's floor plan marked with my targets. Always get to the show early … **be seen, be heard, and be remembered** often throughout the event.

Since I was in publishing/media helping my prospects and clients with market access to their audience, the key was to do homework on the person, the company, the competition, and how I could offer a solution that moved the prospects from conversation to action. When I added value and did not waste time, I stood out from the competition and clearly was seen, heard, and remembered for it. I will share a few secrets on how to accomplish this that worked for me.

Arrive Early and Often!

Let's say you're at an event after a full day on the tradeshow floor, and you want to get there early and stake out a position to **be seen,**

CHAPTER THREE: AUTHENTICITY

be heard, and be remembered. My strategy was to stand near the entrance so I could see who was coming in before they mingled into the crowd. Here a quick stop, handshake, and hello are sometimes good enough to be seen and remembered. When the crowd starts to grow, go find a spot right near the bar! Yes, near the bar, since most of the people will head there at some point. Again, even if you don't talk with many of them, you will be seen and remembered. I always have a rule of meeting at least three new and interesting people that I did not know before I arrive at the event.

TIP: Review the list of speakers, sponsors, and vendors prior to the event to determine if this is an event worth attending. If so, prepare! If not, it's okay to say no if it's not strategically worth your effort—there are plenty of opportunities in the future.

If you don't have a pre-planned target list, then look around the room for someone who looks energetic, approachable, and interesting. Energy is everything! As discussed, know that people attract or detract others with how their energy level is showing up. If you are resonating high energy, people will notice you, feel your energy, and want to connect with you consciously or unconsciously. Come from a place of curiosity; be interested and therefore interesting to others. The opposite applies if you are there for self-interest and gain it will be felt (if not heard) and will detract others from you.

Reframe Networking to Connections!

Fair to say ladies, most women hate networking! It brings a level of anxiety, fear, and frustration with feeling you "have to" network in order to be seen, be heard, and be remembered—whether you are in a corporate environment or an entrepreneur growing your business.

In order for me to be more successful—and "networking" being a critical component of that success—I did a reframe in order to make it work for me. You will see the examples I used below for reframing words that worked better for me. Also, I found—for me, anyway—that the reframed words provided more positive energy for me. Your reframing method could be different; use whatever will help you get over the challenge with networking, since it's a game changer in work and in life.

Networking is connections. This is about building relationships with other people. Be present; be curious to learn about them, and most importantly, how you can help them be successful.

Talking less and asking more. Actively listen to learn more about what is on the person's mind—a burning issue they are trying to resolve, a unique point or two you remember—and use it in a follow-up note within twenty-four to forty-eight hours. It's all about them, not you.

Selling is out—sharing is in! It's a conversation, not a pitch! Ask about them, why they are at the event, others they like to attend, etc. This is a great way to share information and insight about the industry, news, and business opportunities that would help them, not you (yet).

Taking business cards and giving them your attention. There is great opportunity to engage in conversation when you ask them for their business card. Take a moment to look at the card! What do you see that strikes up a conversation i.e. logo, colors, pictures ... anything to acknowledge you are connecting. How many times have you given or received a card and it goes into a pocket? In other countries this would be viewed as

CHAPTER THREE: AUTHENTICITY

disrespectful. It is not until I have received a card do I offer mine as a way to stay connected in the future. If you don't want to stay connected, don't offer your card. If they ask you for your card, by all means give it to them and either make the effort to stay connected or let them make the next move.

Follow up and follow through! Set yourself apart from others and follow up in a timely and unique way. During your conversation, make note of something you heard them say of interest and use it in the follow up. Do your homework before you follow up. Go to LinkedIn or Google and learn more about the person's background and interests. Who in common do you know and who do they know that you would like to know? Of course, if it is about building a business relationship with the person and the company, the company website provides a tremendous resource of information to building out the profile of the company and how you want to follow up with impact.

My personal goal is to get all follow-up notes out within twenty-four hours, and if appropriate, use LinkedIn with a personalized invitation to join your professional network as well. Keep the door open! Remember that people are busy and may not get back to you in the same timely manner! A tip that I use: If I haven't heard back in a few days, I resend an e-mail and put in the subject line, "Hello, Mary White, you may have missed this e-mail!" There is a very good chance you will hear back from them.

Position yourself as the center of influence, the one who knows the movers and shakers. People respond to that, and you'll soon become what you project.
—Bob Burg, author

TIP: Connection Tips

- Prepare, prepare, prepare! Create door-opening questions, either general or specific, about the event you're attending. Actively listen for something to connect with and comment about, sparking a deeper conversation if that's what you want.

- Be energetic, curious, and invested in the conversation by asking questions. Even if you are not feeling energetic—act as if and then become. See more about energy in Chapter Two. Curiosity makes you interested and interesting! If you are going to be there anyway, be present, in the moment, and invested in the experience.

- Stay current with news, events, and the industry! It is a way to have a conversation with people and build relationships.

- Always come from a giving place. Give something of yourself to others—be of service and it will always serve you well and separate you from all the others that are there to network!

- Have enthusiasm and passion: It's contagious! People will see, hear, and remember you!

Relationships

You will never truly know yourself on the strength of your relationships until both have been tested by adversity.
—J.K. Rowling, author

Everything in life includes a relationship whether its with self, with others, or for a desired outcome. How you begin to master awareness and your interpersonal influence (a convincing personal style) is to consciously think before you speak. Be deliberate in the what, how, when, and why you are saying what you are saying. Stay present and in the moment with active listening and less talking. All of this helps you adapt your behavior (still authentically) to the environment, and this translates into being adaptable, present, likeable, trust-worthy, and able to build and maintain strong relationships.

How you handle yourself always is being observed. Ask yourself these questions:

- *Are you calm in a crisis?*
- *Do you recover quickly from mistakes?*
- *Are you speaking up and letting your voice be heard with purpose?*

Composure is a developed skill and is useful in work and life. Even if inside we are feeling out of sync, our exterior position can be developed so we appear composed no matter what. Thinking before you speak helps here.

Another key point worth noting is that people attune to your personal energy level and presence without having to say anything. Remember that our energy shows up in the room before we actually engage with others. We will talk more about the power of personal presence and energy throughout the book.

Connect to others with ease! Ask yourself the following questions:

- *How do you make people feel when you meet them?*
- *Are you present and in the moment, or thinking in your head about what to say next?*
- *Are you comfortable with having a sense of humor, which always helps others to feel more comfortable with ease?*

By helping others to be in the state of being, influence and change is effortless.

Pausing is a great tool to keep handy in any situation. Often we are triggered by what is said or how we react to a situation, and most often it comes from our unconscious level. What I have learned is that our needs drive our behavior—good, bad, or indifferent. Often we are unaware of our needs and expectations and we take things personally. In Chapter Two, in the Energy section, there is a way of learning more about what drains your energy and discovering your personal needs. For now, remember that we always are responding to our needs, and so others are responding to their needs. One of my top needs is respect. Now, respect can mean many different things to others and yet you get to define what it means for you. In my case, being talked over, ignored, or disregarded during a conversation sends my alarm bells screaming. What I have learned to do is to pause and ask myself: What need might this person have when demonstrating these behaviors? Pausing gives me the emotional awareness to know that it is likely not personal, and the other person is often totally unaware of the demonstrated behavior. This person may have the need to be in control, be heard, or be right, and therefore comes to the conversation to meet their personal needs.

The ability for visibility takes work, no two ways about it. It is imperative to **be seen, be heard, and be remembered**, and throughout the book I offer ideas to maintain a constant state of awareness, insight, and knowledge to enhance your A-Game.

Inspired action definitely supports influence with impact. When you walk your talk you are being seen, heard, and remembered. It's implied that you are being your authentic self and demonstrating your personal power and passion.

CHAPTER THREE: AUTHENTICITY

Build Your Entourage

The ideal entourage is composed of influencers and people who are connected to other influencers and achievers. You want to surround yourself with self-sufficient, self-confident, and self-fulfilled individuals.
—Leslie Grossman, author

What's an entourage? I had the pleasure of interviewing and getting to know Leslie Grossman, author of the new book *Link Out: How to Turn Your Network into a Chain of Lasting Connections*. When we spoke prior to her book release, we focused the conversation around building an "entourage" as a new concept on how we connect with others. When one thinks of "entourage" they think about someone like Brad Pitt and Angelina Jolie who have a group that travels the world to serve them; it's all about them!

The new "entourage" is about people that are there to support you, and also how you are supporting them. It's a mutual collaborative relationship where we help each other to succeed and achieve goals and a desired outcome.

Before you begin to build your "entourage," it is important to know who you really are and what defines your personal and professional brand! What makes you unique and different? What are your passions, and most importantly, what do you want people to see and remember about you? Through the process of personal branding, you are creating your story … people remember the story first, and we will talk about this topic further in this chapter.

Grossman asked a great question worth repeating, "Do you know what your family members do?" It is a great way to build an "entourage" with those you think know you or you think you know them. We make a lot of assumptions that people know what we do, and most of the time they don't. Next time there is a family gathering, proactively ask the questions from a place of curiosity such as, "Tell me more about a day in your life at work?"

Or, "I am curious, what is the best part of your job and what do you dislike most?"

Be prepared to share what you do with others. Start off by answering your own questions for you as a way to prepare. Don't be shy about sharing with others what is happening in your world, we all make assumptions that other people already know about us, or only would like to be updated on the latest, or maybe that they would not really care to know! I tried this recently at a gathering, and I did learn something new about each person that was there. In turn, I got a chance to share with them about what was happening with me. And I got an opportunity to change or alter assumptions that people automatically made about me.

Your entourage is made up of people who are connectors! It's all about who they know, what they know, where they are connected, and why they would want to build a relationship with you. That said, when we enter into the process of establishing and building our entourage, it is helpful not to set too many expectations for it. **We don't know what we don't know until we know it.** When we are present and in the moment we are more open, available, and curious about what we are about to see, hear, and remember during the conversations. Many times there will be nuggets of insight and information that can open doors and expand connections where they matter most to you.

When I relocated back to Boston from California I really didn't have an established entourage on this coast. I actively went to several events and organized group events to learn more about those organizations, their membership base, their mission and how it aligned with my personal mission of advancing leadership—and specifically advancing women in business. Let me tell you—building an entourage takes time, effort, money, and focused intention and attention in order to find the right mix to move you into action.

> **TIP:** Find the organizations that matter most to you and join the club. "Okay, then what?" you ask. "How do I become engaged, involved, and figure out how to **be seen, be heard, and be remembered**?" One suggestion is to serve on a committee where you actively participate with others so they learn more about what you say and what you do, building your personal brand each step of the way. When you are with like-minded people, it is effortless to be and stay connected and engaged in the conversation; and the more you give the more you get back naturally.

Your entourage is happy to mentor, sponsor, and introduce you into the right places just as you will do for them. It is a relationship built on trust, insight, knowledge, and desire to serve and support others.

Reciprocity Matters!

This brings me to another topic that is so difficult, for me personally, and for many of the women I coach in my business. That is asking for what you want!

Now let me preface this: when it came to business I had no problem asking for the order. As a matter of fact, I was extremely effective at "asking," and didn't really think much about it. Somehow it was different and difficult for me to personally ask for something I needed. I maintained the attitude *I can take care of this myself!*

I am going to be vulnerable here and share with the world: I don't know how to ask for help, and I downplay it when someone makes the offer! That is crazy and confusing, since most people, including me, would want to help someone ... yet for me accepting the help is a challenge.

I am grateful that Jack, my significant other, happens to be a chief human resource officer and is a tremendously open and gifted resource for me.

With Jack, dialogue is always interesting and profound, and one evening we were talking after dinner, over a glass of wine, about how easy my transition to the East Coast was and how many connections I had made in such a short time. Jack observed and mentioned how many people had called me for help and suggestions, not to mention to attend several "paid" events as a way to grow a network. As we expanded the conversation and talked about a few situations he stopped in mid-sentence and grabbed a piece of paper.

"Here's an exercise I would like you to do, Carole, create an A-B-C-D list of people in your network and put them where you think they belong," he said. So I began to create the different categories of A through D:

A. These were people considered to be a good friend and colleague and we were mutually supportive of each other.

B. People that were solid and have mutual connections that don't require the same consistent connections as the A group, but definitely connect more often than the C group. They would stay on the list, but did not require a consistent connection as the A group did.

C. They were the people that may have had some interest but appeared to be self-focused, yet I was still questioning the longevity of the connection.

D. These were the takers that needed to come off the list! They were just a name I had in my database.

I thought this would be easy and it was not! It was such an "aha" moment, and a turning point for me to really spend time taking a serious look as to who I was spending time with and how many

CHAPTER THREE: AUTHENTICITY

of these relationships were mutually supportive. Since I tended to always want to help others and never ask anyone for help, I didn't realize how much of my time was being spent on giving of me.

It was so profound I took the next several days to dig deeper into the relationships and what was and was not happening. Not to make quick judgments or assumptions about others' intentions, I did take time over the next several weeks to make a conscious connection with the questionable relationships to determine where they would be in the future.

Interestingly enough, several of the names came right off the list; this created more freedom to go about building my relationships differently and more purposefully. I have to say once I made the decision to get serious about this, many new doors opened as I closed out the old.

I paid particular attention to the words that were said (see the "Words We Use Matter" section under the Communications chapter), and if these were more "I" and "I need" or "I could really use" statements more than, "how can I help" and "what can I do for you" (reciprocity language) there was a ping in my stomach. Delving deeper to hear more I found when the conversation was all about "them" with little regard to me, it became clear that this was more of an acquaintance instead of a relationship.

Much to my surprise, there were far more "take" dynamics than I would have expected or desired. However, it was a huge opportunity for me to begin to shift where and how I spent my time and what were the qualities in my current and future relationships that mattered most.

It took some time to go through this process and commit to the relationships that mattered most where I focused not only attention, but true authenticity by showing up open, honest, and being okay with expressing vulnerability. I shared with each person this "aha" moment and exercise and how much their relationship mattered to me.

Now it was time to start working on asking for help, and I felt I had a group of people that it would be safe to share my vulnerability around the "asking." More importantly, it was time to start learning how to accept openly what others wanted to do for me. What began to happen was the conversations shifted from me as the "helper" to a mutual exchange of give and take—with far more enriching and rewarding relationships being developed at a deeper level.

I have been moving with baby-steps here, and am committed to keep taking steps until it is more comfortable and natural for me. It is still not where it needs to be; a few of my close, dear friends are reminding me when I am not practicing what I preach. I am happily accepting their feedback.

We all operate primarily at an unconscious level that has been built around most everything we have seen, heard, or remembered in life. Think about a huge computer that stores everything for the future, and how the database of knowledge, insight, beliefs, limited beliefs, attitudes, judgments, and decisions are based on past experiences known or unknown consciously. The more you can be curious about seeing things differently and asking yourself "what if" questions the more conscious choices you can make.

Rejection!

*There's nothing like rejection
to make you do an inventory of yourself.*
—James Lee Burke, author

"We don't know what we don't know until we know it" has been used throughout the book. It was used once again through the previous exercise, and with the shift I had around my relationships it was amazing to see what I did not know; and what was right in front of me the entire time. It was not until I was ready to "see" did it appear.

This happens anytime we can bring an unconscious thought, feeling, or belief into consciousness (also known as awareness). I did not know what I didn't know about my fear of rejection. If I asked for something and someone would say "no"—rejection! This fear went way back to when I was a little girl and had my voice limitations. I would ask a question and no one would hear me, or it would be dismissed or denied, building up my adversity to rejection!

Even though I am committed and continue to do the deep, personal development, these emotions are at the core of my being, and still create an emotional charge when I am faced with them. Rejection is one of the toughest situations people find themselves in. It's inevitable! You don't get the job you wanted. The person you are attracted to is not attracted to you. Ask for something you really want and the answer is "no." It is difficult and painful when it happens. Yet, we make a choice to stay in the pain or evolve to a different place.

So I give myself the gift to go for more of the "asking," and stretch out of my comfort zone whenever there is an opportunity to face the possibility of rejection, knowing it is not about me necessarily, and I don't take it personally. It is just another moment in time and this will change, guaranteed!

Throughout life we mask these fears and others by not asking for what we want or dealing with the potential outcome; in my case this is known as "rejection."

When we think we have accomplished a deep level of awareness and acceptance of something that got in our way, and check it off the list, there then is a deeper and more meaningful learning that shows up for us. It's the gift that keeps giving!

Imposter Syndrome!

Whether you think you can or you think you can't, either way you—are right.
—Henry Ford, inventor

"Imposter Syndrome" is another big area of struggle for many of us no matter where we are on our life's journey. When I made the decision to leave my corporate life and start my own business helping to advance women, and a few good men, to find and use the power of voice and choice, the "Imposter Syndrome" was a big neon sign over my personal billboard.

Think about this for a minute. I was going to help others find their voice and choice when I had serious voice limitations! I would be in the front of the room telling others how to use their voice when I couldn't. The power of voice (What power? It was barely a whisper!) and choice; what was I thinking on this one? Talk about limited beliefs and not-being-worthy self-talk not just holding me back, but stopping me dead in my tracks.

I was frustrated with the desire versus the reality of the physical limitations I had to deal with. *Wait a minute; I have spent the last many years being very successful using my voice. What am I saying to myself?* The self-talk dialog went back and forth often, until I stepped up and out, and faced my fear of rejection or being "found out." Fortunately, since the surgery, I don't have as many negative moments around the power of voice and choice, and have become very comfortable showing up in my authentic way and trusting it will be good enough.

In my experience with shifting from connecting with people, to building relationships that matter, I realized that you don't need a lot of people in your entourage, you need the right people. Being in sales for most of my professional career I lived with a "competitive mindset" because that's all I knew. As I discovered more about my authentic self the competitive mindset clearly was something I could do easily and effortlessly, but it brought up a more negative energy level for me. Or another way of putting it—it gave me an adrenaline rush, and this was not sustainable for me long term. (We will talk more about this in Chapter Four: Alliances/Common-Unity.)

What aligns more with who I am becoming is being in a "collaborative mindset," although most of us are not conditioned to collaborate with each other. It's finding a new language, appreciation, and understanding on being in collaboration without defaulting to our natural and nurtured tendency.

CHAPTER THREE: AUTHENTICITY

You can make more friends in two months by becoming more interested in other people than you can in two years trying to get people interested in you.
—Dale Carnegie, author

TIP: The differentiation between a network and an entourage and ways to work with them:

Networking Strategies	Entourage Strategies
Brief connections/small talk	Long-term relationships
Get all the business cards you can	People you are connected with consistently
Forgets your name when they see you again	Available, responsive to your e-mails and calls
One-way dialog and support	Support each other at multiple touch-points
Vague and meaningless conversation	In-depth, meaningful, and valuable conversation
Inconsistent if any follow-up	Reliable follow-up and follow-through
Contacts you when they need something	Initiates introductions and referrals
Selfishly-motivated attitude	Win/win/win attitude
Not interested in your personal life	Interested in your personal and professional life
A casual acquaintance value set	Trusted and honored relationships

The Difference Between a Mentor and a Sponsor and Why It Matters!

Ask for what you want and be prepared to get it.
—Maya Angelou, author and poet

I am so grateful to have interviewed and established a strong connection with some of the experts in the area of leadership—and specifically in the area of advancing women through the power of sponsorship. Betsy Myers, founding director of Bentley University's Center for Women and Business conducts a series of best practice forums that cover this topic, women's leadership, and Gender Intelligence. Rebecca Shambaugh—author of *It's Not a Glass Ceiling, It's a Sticky Floor* and the recently released *Make Room for Her*—and I had a conversation about this and I incorporated some of what we discussed here.

Mentors and sponsors are relevant, timely, and needed, especially for employees wanting to advance forward in their career and business. Let's break it down:

> A *mentor* is a valuable resource and role model that offers advice and counsel, provides perspective and constructive criticism as support for you.

> A *sponsor* takes it to the next level and is willing to advocate on your behalf with respect to advancement and strategic opportunities. Sponsorship means that someone at a high enough level believes in you and is influential, trusted, and willing to commit to helping you advance your role. As you move through the leadership pipeline it is critical to align yourself with the right people to help advance your career.

CHAPTER THREE: AUTHENTICITY

Without sponsorship, both men and women are likely to be overlooked for promotions, regardless of competence or readiness. This is particularly key in upper management and in the C-Suite where there is competition for promotion.

Recent research indicates that men are more naturally sponsored by senior executives and that high-potential women are over-mentored and under-sponsored relative to their male counterparts. This is a clear indication of why they are not advancing as quickly as desired.

While women are known for their ability to build and nurture relationships, they fail to cultivate and invest in relational capital at the executive levels. Here are a few tips that could turn this around.

Hard work doesn't get you promoted! Who you know, who knows you, what your current role is and what your long-term, desired career path may be is a factor in attracting a sponsor.

Cultivate a rich and diverse network! Include both male and female executives. Build relationships with key decision makers that will ensure you get the training, development, and connections that move you forward in your career.

Be prepared to be sponsored! You need to know what you want in terms of your career goals. Create a list that includes the things you enjoy doing the most; including your natural talents and how they fit into your short- and long-term career goals. What is your ability to take on stretch goals that include some risk? Are you willing to step out of your comfort zone and learn something new? What would you want to learn about someone before you would sponsor them? Be sure to prepare beyond whatever might be asked so you will be conscious of the direction and path you want to take.

Consider potential sponsors! They might be in your network, or those that need to be added to your network. Sponsors should be connected at the senior level, influential in the ranks, and be an ambassador for you. I had a mentor that ultimately became my sponsor. I didn't know at the time that he was promoting me and my abilities into the C-Suite as a high-potential player for the organization and the industry. The role from mentor, where he was guiding me, to sponsorship, where he was advocating on behalf of me, required of us both a different and focused intention around the new relationship.

Mentor and Sponsor Roles

A **mentor** is someone who is focused on you and your development. They are willing to share insights and knowledge that can guide you and help with resources and connections. They serve as a role model, and help you navigate the corporate landscape. They help you come to decisions that move you forward without telling you what or how to do it. And mentors can be part of a short-term or long-term relationship.

I have mentored women for the past ten years through professional organizations in a structured format, as well as through individual mentoring situations where I could add value and support in a specific way. Both situations start with establishing a goal for the engagement. Rules of engagement can be commitment, communication, and honesty. And the role of mentor is to support, not do the work. The mentee is the one that drives the relationship, direction, and desire.

A **sponsor** is a senior-level professional and connected enough to open doors for you. They help pave the way, make connections to senior leaders, and help promote visibility for you when you are not there. They look for and help cultivate career opportunities. They provide honest and candid feedback and advise you where you need to go. You are responsible to make it happen. The sponsor puts a tremendous amount of faith in you and expects that you step up to meet it.

I found that when my mentor moved to being a sponsor, both of our commitments to the relationship shifted. I had to be more intentional and strategic to not only step up to meet expectations, but to create my goals and focus for the short- and long-term. I had to know my unique value proposition and follow up and follow through on assignments. Many of them were stretch assignments—way out of my comfort zone—that carried a high-risk factor that could fail, and fail in public.

Unique Value Proposition

What is your Unique Value Proposition? A statement that is clear, concise, and specific regarding what uniquely your value is offering: i.e. credibility, reputation, trust, quality, accountability that is 100-percent accurate and instantly credible. Speak from your heart and soul when you are creating what is uniquely you.

How to begin creating your UVP starts where you are internally. What do you value about yourself? What differentiates you from others? Why would people want to connect and work with you? Then refine, rewrite, and rework a statement until it resonates effortlessly with you.

Proactively engage and develop these relationships! Once identified, then build a strategic plan on how to cultivate and build the relationship (it doesn't happen overnight). They need to get to know you, your career aspirations, and your unique value proposition, and you need to provide them with the insight, knowledge, and information they need to feel prepared to sponsor you. After all, they are putting their reputation on the line, and the more we prepare them for what we want them to think, feel, and act on the better win/win/win outcome.

When engaging with a sponsor you need to be prepared prior to the asking! Ask yourself these questions:

> *Are you clear on what success looks like to you?*
> *Do you know your talents, strengths, passions, purpose?*
> *Have you set short- and long-term goals for your work and life?*
> *Do you know your Unique Value Proposition?*
> *What have you done to stay visible in the past?*
> *Who are the people in your network today? Who needs to be in there for the future?*
> *Are you willing to get out of your comfort zone?*
> *Are you open to men being a sponsor and open to their candid feedback?*

Ask for what you want! Tory Johnson, CEO of Women For Hire, shared great insight on this topic: "[Women] still have this idea that if we just do a good job, someone's going to tap us on the shoulder and reward us with a promotion. That so rarely happens! It's up to you and you alone to put together a plan, and then rally the right people to sponsor you."

When you ask for help, clarity is important. When we are clear, yes comes easier than no. Many times the answer no is because the person is not clear on what you are asking or if they can help you. The more specific and direct, the easier it is for someone to say yes. What are you looking for? Why? Why you? Why now? Why are you asking them?

It is important to be clear on expectations and agreements of the sponsor/sponsor-ee relationship before you begin so there are no misunderstandings. I have found that people, especially executives, are willing to help when you are clear, articulate, and direct with what you need. No one can read your mind, see what you do, or even imagine the "what if" possibilities. You have to tell, ask, and support them with the information.

So how do you get started?

CHAPTER THREE: AUTHENTICITY

It may feel like a repeat performance, yet it is exactly what we need—to constantly be circling back whenever we desire change in our work and life. Here are a few suggestions on how to get started.

- Be clear on what you are looking for in your career and the next steps and the action steps you need to take.

- Use the SMART goal process to strategically plan who, what, when, where, and why you should be "sponsored."

- Tap into your "entourage" both inside and outside the organization for feedback and guidance before you approach your potential "sponsors."

- How's the visibility of You, Inc.? Are you out there at industry events, company events, and networking events so you are being seen, heard, and remembered? Are you expressing your unique value proposition wherever the opportunity presents itself?

- Are you comfortable with some risk and able to demonstrate it?

- Have you identified two or three potential "sponsors" that can help you get where you want to get in an organized and structured fashion?

- Do your SMART goals include how you will make the connection with each of the potential "sponsors?"

Answering these questions will better prepare you to "ask" for what you want and build the confidence to make the connections you need.

BUILD YOUR A-GAME

The Art of Negotiation!

*Let us never negotiate out of fear,
but let us never fear to negotiate.*
—John F. Kennedy, 35th American president

Okay ... I say "negotiation" and you say what? Feel what? And do you know why? Full transparency here—I love to negotiate and view it as an art form and a communication style that moves people into action and results with a win/win/win outcome. That was not always the case, and over the years of navigating the business world, I mastered the art of negotiation and learned through many challenging situations how to hone this communication skill in work and life.

Life is a series of negotiations starting with the minute you wake up and make the decision like *Do I get out of bed when the alarm goes off or opt to stay in bed for another five minutes?* Or when you have a workout scheduled and opt to jump onto e-mail instead. At work, do you participate in the meeting or sit quietly and observe? You have a huge project to implement; do you take the time to schedule out the process or just dive right in, adjusting along the way? We are constantly negotiating with ourselves.

Do you feel you are successful at making a decision or choice? Then you have mastered the art of negotiation at the core. You see, we often get stuck on the word—and expectation of the word— "negotiation." And unfortunately, there are still second-generation gender biases around "negotiating" as women. Here's what Professor Deborah Kolb, PhD, well-known authority on gender issues and negotiations, has to say on this topic:

"New leaders fail at an impressive rate. That's because many people don't know how to negotiate for what they need to improve their odds of success."

In Kolb's research, they found that women—who negotiate conditions for their success as leaders—had higher performance

CHAPTER THREE: AUTHENTICITY

reviews, were more satisfied with their jobs, and less likely to leave their companies than women who did not negotiate conditions for their success. "Often overlooked are valuable opportunities to jump-start their leadership because of three faulty assumptions: 'My choice is either yes or no,' 'My appointment speaks for itself,' and, 'I can pick up the slack.'" Before you can build a strategic campaign to negotiate your career conditions, you need to perform well in a new role, and you must overcome these assumptions.

I was fortunate to be offered promotions throughout my career and all of them were stretch assignments; yet I too had these assumptions. My immediate internal reaction to each opportunity was: *I should say no, because I have never done this before and it's going to impact my life dramatically.* My next feeling of: *Be careful for what you wish for, now you have the chance to fail or succeed.* And then, of course, I thought I had to do it all without asking for support along the way.

I talked earlier about becoming the publisher on a troubled magazine after serving on the sales leadership team for six years, and over those years I felt I was clearly the right person to turn the magazine around, yet management continued to hire in new men to try and fix the problem. Candidly, I resented some of their decisions and was frustrated I did not get the opportunity. Why did it take so long? Second-generation bias was clearly the reason. The company was run by men. All the leadership positions were held by men and there was a solid "boys' club" mentality throughout the organization. Women were in supportive roles with the exception of the sales organization. Women were not expected to negotiate on behalf of themselves and it was frowned on if you did. Believe me, I got labeled over the years as "aggressive," "bold," and "ballsy" every time I negotiated on something.

I was offered the job! Now what?

I assumed that the appointment to publisher would speak for itself and that people would accept that I was perfect for the role. Otherwise why did they give it to me? I was far from perfect, but equally established and qualified as others in the role to make the strategic decisions for success based on hands-on market conditions and client expectations. My market and customer knowledge was the foundation of setting realistic expectations with the leadership team and to ensure some room to implement much-needed and time-sensitive changes.

Being visible in the different circles once exclusive to the men was a point that needed to be negotiated, and I needed help from the CEO to open those doors across the organization locally and globally. He was the one to champion the decision to offer me this role and give me the financial support needed to implement real change.

I was offered this opportunity because I had what the company needed, and they finally realized that I was indeed the best candidate to turn this book around if at all possible. Even though I knew a lot about the industry and the history of the publication, I did not know that much about running the details of the business finances, editorial design, and back-office procedures. Before I said yes, I gathered as much information and insight on what resources I would need to make the changes needed. Part of this process was to know the gaps; such as the skills needed for certain aspects of the role or lack of hands-on experience to date, and more about the resources—such as access to training or experts already established in the industry or organization, and how to tap into them for additional support that would not take away from my budget. I had to understand the pay scale based on market data was key for negotiating with knowledge. I tapped into key people and asked for their help if I took this position, and fortunately this move eliminated surprise and ultimately added support that helped me succeed along the way.

All of this was part of the negotiation process of getting to a yes AND the position. If I hadn't taken the time to research and leverage, it could have been a lost opportunity well into the future. When it was time to give my answer, I felt more prepared and in the driver's

CHAPTER THREE: AUTHENTICITY

seat as a result of all the research I had done, and came to the table detached from emotions and armed with a more fact-based dialog.

The negotiations included setting realistic expectations for success, which included a guaranteed time frame before they could opt out of the agreement. It also included the stipulation that I did not have to relocate back to the home office to conduct my role (the first time that happened in the company). We negotiated that there wouldn't be micromanagement of the changes for at least six months to gain traction in the market (hands-off from scrutiny of every little thing).

They aligned me with a great financial manager inside to assist me in the areas where I needed to grow, without judgment. The CEO personally campaigned inside and outside the organization in support of his decision and for me in this new role. I was able to negotiate a substantial marketing budget to support these changes in the marketplace. And, I was able to negotiate a pay package that I knew for a fact was what others had been paid in the past (I researched the market and actual trends), and lastly, I knew I had my boss's back for the dramatic impact we were about to make, and he trusted me to implement it.

So why did this work out the way it did for my strategy? Effective leaders develop a sense of purpose that aligns with their personal values and advances the collective good. They look beyond the status-quo to what is possible, and give a compelling reason to take action despite personal fears and insecurities. Good leaders are seen as authentic and trustworthy because we are willing to take risks in the service and support of shared goals. We connect and collaborate with others to the larger purpose, inspire commitment, demonstrate resilience and resolve, and help others find a deeper meaning in their work. It's in an integrated leadership process that goes beyond one individual. And sometimes is a challenge for women, who must establish credibility in a culture that is deeply conflicted about whether, when, and how they should exercise authority.

The Gender Differences

> *If someone believes they are limited by gender, race or background they will become limited.*
> —Carly Fiorina, American business executive

Victoria Pynchon and Lisa Gates, authors of the *She Negotiates* blog, have this to say about the gender difference: "Gender bias is silent, subtle, and damaging and the place gender bias is most deeply and secretly lodged is inside ourselves." This applies to men and women even though it has its differences; that said, it is not good or bad, just different.

"Second-generation bias is embedded in stereotypes and organizational practices that can be hard to detect but when people are made aware of it, they see the opportunity for change," cites Kolb. With awareness then comes choice on how we wish to contribute to the change we want to see in the world. This is an opportunity to make a difference by speaking up on something that does not feel authentic or right for you. Be willing to pause and self-reflect on what your silent biases might be and change this filter in the process. Remember that we have unconscious filters that can only change with awareness and choice.

Most women I worked with and have coached that have been in the workforce for more than twenty-plus years were unaware of personally having been victims of gender discrimination, and many women have worked hard to take gender out of the equation. They want to be recognized for their skills and talents and contributions.

In my coaching business I work with professional women today that still feel that they have no power to determine their own success. What holds them back?

"I don't feel connected either positive or negative with the guys I work with. They are nice but don't include me in the decision process very often. When I offer my thoughts they are disregarded."

CHAPTER THREE: AUTHENTICITY

"There is great intention to provide the women in the organization leadership training programs, but it seems that when a leadership role opens, there are no women on the list. When asked about it, they say they can't find a female candidate with the skills and experience to fill the role."

Many of the biases are a result of leaders who tend to hire and promote people, mainly men, whose backgrounds and careers resemble their own. Men have written the job descriptions and criteria for the roles. It is known that men will go for the role, even if they don't meet all the requirements, while women tend to hold back until they are 100 percent sure of success.

I had conversations with several of my human resource executive associates and asked their feedback on this and here's what I heard:

"Women fail to thrive and reach their full potential when they opt to take a staff position to accommodate family matters."

"They don't raise their hand for stretch assignments."

"When asked to take on more responsibility, the answer is often 'no' because they can't put in any more hours than they already are doing."

"They are too nice to make the tough decisions needed for change."

"Cooperation is more meaningful than competition, and sometimes we need to compete."

Personally speaking, I recognized the pervasive gender bias, and that motivated me because I could take action to counter it (not easily or effectively at times) and that was a personal mission of mine in the corporate world. I was able to seek out mentors and sponsors to navigate the waters and over time negotiate a working relationship that fit both my professional and personal values and goals.

TIP: Seek out those mentors and sponsors that can help you connect to stretch assignments, and ask for help. Raise your hand even when you feel fear of failure; you never know if you don't try and remember, you can't grow sitting on the sidelines.

Time to ASK!

It is your life—but only if you make it so.
—Eleanor Roosevelt, American first lady

I interviewed fantastic women on my radio show *The AWE Factor* and want to include some of the great nuggets shared on core negotiation strategies. Victoria Pynchon and Lisa Gates collaborate as authors and co-founders of *She Negotiates*, an online resource that actively helps women embrace negotiations in work and life.

"Negotiation is conversation leading to agreement," is their tagline, and what a great reframe of a word that conjures up fear and uncertainty. Here are some of the "Negotiation 101" tips featured on *She Negotiates* to ponder:

- Determine your worth. It's best to land on a number versus a range. Base it on market research, your accomplishments, and your future potential. Aim high with starting salary. Go beyond salary and include benefits as part of the package.

CHAPTER THREE: AUTHENTICITY

Women don't negotiate their salaries early in their careers, which ultimately makes it difficult to catch up down the road. We leave upwards of a million dollars or more on the table throughout our careers. Be sure to negotiate vacation time, flex time, or what other requirements you have utilizing the benefits options.

- Push for a performance review at the start and ask: How are performance reviews handled? How often? What are the metrics used for performance reviews? What are the specific expectations leading to advancement? A few things happen here. First, it shows you take this role very seriously and want to be successful. Second, you are letting them know you are serious about advancing your career in the organization. Third, it demonstrates your savvy leadership skills during the interview process.

- If you go ask for a raise and they say no, ask to revisit the option in three or six months and "rock it" during that timeframe. Evaluate your workload and look at the original job description and rewrite it to reflect and align with your current job today. Then benchmark your new position. (Check out Payscale.com as a resource.) The value of this exercise is twofold. You are assessing your role and responsibilities and how they might be different than what was originally expected, and you have new and actual data to share with your boss on how the role has evolved since you started. We assume people know and see what we are doing, and the chances are slim to none that they do—until we share it with them. It is up to us to inform others on our expectations and why.

- If you want to telecommute, negotiate a telecommute agreement! Don't fall into the trap of taking a pay cut because of perceived fewer hours as a result—negotiate for your current full salary. Shift your employer's thinking from hours spent in your work to the results you are producing for the organization.

More and more men are looking for telecommuting deals, and you can be assured they would not settle for a pay cut nor would it likely be offered. Assume the same position.

- Always negotiate salary when you start or take on new duties or a promotion. Discuss pay anytime there is a lateral move, change of career, or transition from employee to contractor. Don't assume a lateral move means the same job responsibilities. Do your research before you say yes—it's hard to negotiate after you say yes. It is better to take time to reflect before you automatically accept an offer, as this too is part of a negotiation strategy. Holding out gives you more power in the conversation instead of fear that if you wait the offer might go away. They obviously see value in what you can do for them, trust this and use this time to negotiate for you.

- Cardinal rule: Never negotiate against yourself by saying, "I am asking for X but am willing to negotiate." If you want to signal flexibility, demonstrate it by putting other compensation elements on the table such as travel, continued education, vacation etc. For example, "I am asking for four weeks of vacation time, but I am flexible in requiring that."

Visit www.SheNegotiates.com for worksheets and resources to aid you in your negotiation efforts.

"Nice Girls Just Don't Get It"

> *Think highly of yourself because the words take you at your own estimate.*
> —unknown

Dr. Lois Frankel is the author of several *Nice Girl* books that really speak to the heart of our limited beliefs and self-sabotaging behaviors, and provides assessments, insights, and a great wit on how to get out of our own way.

I interviewed Frankel for my radio show; we had a tremendous connection and were on the same page throughout our interview. Frankel's passion, as is mine, is: the empowerment of women and girls that don't have or use their voice and create choices for themselves.

We talked about a few of Frankel's "101 Mistakes" and one would be not leveraging relationships. Frankel says, "Women need to understand inherent to every relationship there is a quid pro quo—there's one thing in exchange for another." Often women only are using half the equation when people ask them for something. They gladly do it, but don't ask for anything back. I have been guilty of this most of my life.

Number one: *Assess your past and don't let it get in the way of your present or your future; that you can rewrite the script.* Think about when you use a tape recorder; you record, listen, don't like what you hear and re-record until you get it just right. This is the same process internally with the same results—a desired outcome.

Number two: *Women tend to use too many words and as a result don't get heard.* "Oh, yes, thank you for your time and I am grateful to be here and what I want to talk about is well, you know, important stuff!" Way too much, we need to get to the point quickly.

Number three: *Women ask for permission and men ask for forgiveness.* When women are asked for something that needs to be done that is humanly impossible to get done—women get it done. Men, on the other hand, negotiate. They will set realistic expectations regarding staffing, budgeting, and timing for delivery of the project before they accept the situation.

There was a University of California, Irvine Graduate School of Management study conducted by Professor Lisa Barron that found 85% of men were comfortable with equating their worth with a dollar amount, and they knew what they were worth. But 83% percent of the women remarked they were less comfortable equating a dollar value, and that their employer was responsible for determining their worth! In the study, there were thirty-eight MBA students that went through a mock interview process. Each started with a salary offer of $61,000. Men "asked" for $68,556 on average while women "requested" $67,000 for the same job.

Now the numbers were not that dramatically different, but the mind-set and belief systems differed greatly. Barron's study found gaps between the way men and women describe themselves in negotiations at the time when salaries are determined. Men apparently felt more entitled to earn more money. One male graduate stated, "I am not a typical entry employee," and another said, "I am not a standard student, and I don't think that I should be categorized in the same range of capability and therefore salary." Female students said very different things such as, "I am very similar to my peers," and another said "As long as I am making the average, that's all I really care about."

And some of my female coaching clients have expressed comments such as: "I need to prove myself first before they will pay me more," and, "I am new in the business world and haven't earned my stripes," and, "I am making enough to be comfortable and money is only part of my motivation to work."

Do you see a pattern here ladies? It is time to change this dynamic—taking small wins in the right direction.

Visit Chapter Five for more on the topic of wealth and being "rich." The link here is that many women want to just be comfortable; they don't want to be rich. You need to define "rich" or "wealth" for yourself. I only ask that you include the mindset of being comfortable enough to not fear living, asking, and creating the desired life you deserve.

What's in Your W.A.L.L.E.T.?

Once you create a choice about what it is YOU want in life, you can then—and only then—begin to create the outcome. This takes us out of the "wishing," "wondering," or "hoping" state and puts us in a place of awareness and action.

Dr. Lois Frankel shares her W.A.L.L.E.T. principles and I'm adding my take-a-ways from our conversation:

W – Write down what you want people to say about you in twenty-five words or less. You decide the messaging you want people to hear and repeat when they think of you. But do you know what they are saying? It is time to get feedback to shape and implement what it is you want others to know and say about you.

A – Apply actionable behaviors. Act on the vision statement you create for yourself and for others to "see." If the video camera can't see it, it won't be captured … you have to let people know what you want them to "see." The words we use matter—make this action-oriented in a way that helps people to resonate with your energy and what you want them to feel by what you say and do.

L – Look to the edge. Don't make your brand too safe! Too many people play in the middle where it is safe. Those who play at the edge with some risk and first-mover advantages get noticed and rewarded! It is okay to step out of your comfort zone and try living on the edge. For example, look for and accept a stretch assignment that takes you out of the middle of the pack, and one that will demonstrate your willingness to take calculated risks. You will be rewarded for growth and expansion in your role. It does pay off.

L – Let others know about it! We often believe that our hard work and efforts get noticed and people can automatically "see" what we are doing. They can't, and it is up to us to share what we want them to know. This is all about using your voice in a way to inform, and not brag, about what you are doing by using a story format. For example, "This assignment has deepened my knowledge on how to best deliver the product earlier than projected. I was able to shave off thirty days in the process by changing roles within the team while aligning them more with their natural talents." This step alone is a game changer to getting more of what you want in life. There is a great book, *Brag! The Art of Tooting Your Own Horn without Blowing It* by Peggy Klaus; it's worth reading.

E – Elicit 360 feedback! This is a great tool to assess what others "see" in you. What you are doing well, what you could be doing more of—AND what people don't even recognize: what you believe you are representing out there. Oftentimes it is difficult to have the mirror put up for you, yet it is the turning point to shape YOUR choices. This could be handled formally or informally—asking those who know you well and you trust to be honest about what they see.

T – Treat others with abundance! When we come from a place of abundance we operate at a different vibration. There is more than enough for everyone—when you believe it and act "as if" you become it! A scarcity mindset delivers exactly what you think about and cuts off access to amazing opportunities. For example: "That will never happen for me because I don't have an MBA." Or, "Everyone is already doing this; there is nothing left for me to do differently, so forget about it." Is your cup half empty or half full?

Remember that negotiation is a communication tool intended to move someone or something into action with a win/win/win result. You already have mastered the basics, and here is an opportunity to expand and develop these skills to advance your career and purpose further. Being comfortable with asking for what you want and going for it will set you up for more success and more positive results just by asking. Take time to notice the limited beliefs when they show up, pause, and reframe them so they work for you and not against you. We stop ourselves more than others stop us, and as you build and bring your A-Game to the world, this will be a natural process at the unconscious competent level.

Resilience–Building Your Bounce Back!

> *Fall down seven, stand up eight.*
> —Japanese proverb

Have you ever wondered how some people are resilient and have the ability to bounce back even in the face of adversity? And there are others that fall victim to their surroundings, situations, and challenging experiences in work and life. So, are people born with resiliency? Does everyone already have this capability?

My experience and understanding is that we are all born with the capacity to develop, build, and change anything, and yes, resiliency is like a muscle that you build up over time by using it with focus and intention to change an outcome.

I have experienced many opportunities to build resiliency since I was a little girl. You read my story in the introduction of my open-heart surgery and the limitations that came with it and the fact that I was raised in a large family environment with no shortage of drama, challenges, and obstacles. And of course my working life was "Adversity University" from where I earned every degree it was passing out to its students. Adversity was my normal! As a result, I built up tremendous bounce-back strength that required self-awareness, self-discovery, self-acceptance, and self-worth. I also mentioned spending twenty-five plus years in the male-dominated publishing industry, and had the opportunity to advance up the ranks to the "glass ceiling" that finally closed in on me. And over the years there were so many challenges and facing-adversity moments that if I did not have the ability to bounce back, I would have been bounced out. Most of the time, I was not consciously aware of how I faced some of these challenges, I just knew at the core that I was stronger than the situation and that kept me moving forward. There were times that I pushed forward only to fall backward into old patterns or beliefs. Without breakdowns (and there were plenty) we cannot break through, and ultimately move that breakdown point forward, forever preparing us for different breakthrough moments.

Back in 2012, I had an opportunity to coauthor a chapter in the *Savvy Leadership Strategies for Women* book, which totally aligned with my work in helping to advance women as they built their A-Game in work and life. When I heard about the opportunity I had an immediate "yes" reaction. I wanted in on the project and spoke with the publisher. The good news: I could participate. The bad news was I had three weeks to turn it around. And the worst news: I was leaving for a vacation to Mexico the next day!

"No worries," I said, "I can make it happen," and I immediately went into "freeze" mode. My left-brain thinking was telling me to organize my thoughts and to find research and facts from my experience. *Great, there is plenty of it, what do I choose?* My right-brain thinking was all about the creative process: how to best communicate my message, and collaborate with nineteen others to bring the leadership voice out there. No-brain thinking was, "Huh ... what were you thinking?" and "The timing is not good, and now I don't have the option to back out and not do it." Whole-brain thinking was able to take the logic and emotion along with a pause for reflection—to trust the process and that it would come together, and I would find the right directive and expression to bring forth a

CHAPTER THREE: AUTHENTICITY

meaningful message. Aha! Trusting the process is oftentimes difficult for someone who is very results oriented, and during these times really letting go and being with the present moment takes a big leap of faith. The good news is that faith wins out more times than not.

I was sitting on the beach in Mexico, totally enjoying the relaxation of the midday cocktail hour and catching up on my reading. Jack was curious as to how I could be so calm, and not be spending the entire vacation meeting the deadline for the chapter that was due. Why, because I had no idea what I was going to write about, so I was avoiding it.

As the week was passing by quickly, I found myself watching the palm trees blow in the high winds off the ocean and how they served a purpose of shading and providing a breeze from the heat of the sun. They would bend and not break, just like people in the midst of change. This resonated with me and made me think of the savvy leaders in the stormy business climates we were experiencing those days. Imagine working in eye of the storm with 100-mile-an-hour, hurricane-force winds from the overstressed leadership team, and think to yourself: *What and who will be standing if we get through this situation?* I was able to reflect on my former leadership teams and quickly identified the leader who talked a big game but avoided conflict; and another leader who had a lot to say but did not deliver on what they promised. I had thought, "Someday, you are going to be found out that you are an empty suit that says all the right things to keep you in this job!" When 100 mile-an-hour winds hit, these were the people that would not be standing in the end.

That was my life, and that would be my chapter: "Leadership in the PALM of Your Hand." Then synchronicity arrived when I was walking by the free poolside book shelf and picked up a washed-out, hardcover book. I flipped the pages, and what did I come to but a story about Hurricane Ike in Texas in 2008, written by Joel Osteen, television minister and author of *It's Your Time*. I happen to like Joel Osteen's work and when I opened up to this story it was a clear message that this was my palm tree connection.

The Hurricane Ike story talked about how the only tree that does not get blown down or uprooted during a hurricane was the palm tree. The palm was able to bend so that it did not break, and was able to have the top touch the ground, but when the wind died down it bounced back stronger than ever ... now that is resilience! Science shows us that when a palm is being pushed and bent over, its root system is actually strengthening, giving it new opportunity to grow. As leaders of our lives, we always are building this muscle when faced with change or uncertainty, so that the muscle is always present when needed.

Just like the savvy leader who is able to weather the storm, these leaders also know it is temporary, it takes time to appreciate their resilience and grace while recognizing the opportunity to grow and expand their personal power, passion, and purpose in work and life. I love acronyms and created the "Leadership in the PALM of Your Hand" chapter around three different sets of PALM principles. They include:

Principle #1: **P**roactively demonstrate how your company can leverage your talents to achieve bottom-line results. **A**ddress challenges and overcome obstacles. **L**everage your drive, knowledge, and relationships to achieve measurable results. **M**aximize opportunities to learn and grow professionally and be successful.

Principle #2: **P**ersevere with passion, purpose, and possibilities. **A**spire to authenticity and openness when you inform, involve, and engage the business, strategy, and people. **L**ead by example and keep moving forward with courage, convictions, and commitment. **M**entor, motivate, and create memorable moments that matter.

Principle #3: **P**ay attention in the present moment in order to change course and shift direction as needed. **A**ct after

CHAPTER THREE: AUTHENTICITY

understanding because **you don't know what you don't know until you know it**, and only then can you take action. Listen, learn, and lead with empathy, understanding, and respect for others at all times. Motivate and engage with a sense of humor.

You can find more information about *Savvy Leadership Strategies for Women* on my website.

I talk about self-awareness in building your A-Game, and this is the first stepping stone to resiliency. You have to know what your core values are and what is driving you from deep within. This is often an unconscious action until we make it a conscious awareness. Understanding our values, needs, and desires are like the rudder of a ship steering us where we need to go—whether we like it or not—it is the core of authenticity.

Self-discovery is when you are doing the deep questioning of who, what, when, where, and why—either situational or in general—utilizing the left-brain, right-brain, no-brain, whole-brain thinking process. *Self-acceptance*, whatever you are currently experiencing, acts as the polar opposite of resistance, and will attract more of which you desire. We know we cannot change others, only how we choose to respond in any given situation. We should trust that we make the right decision in the moment, and we have the free will and the ability to make different choices whenever we choose to do so.

Self-worth (the one we will be working and honing our entire lives) is when we set personal boundaries that we won't let others cross, and they are oftentimes in conflict with our core values. Self-worth is our honor, our integrity, our word, and our true authentic selves. When you honor self you cannot lose in any situation. It may feel like you are losing at the time, but with time and reflection you will realize just how much you've gained as a result of adversity and how you faced it.

"Road to Resilience"

Once we believe in ourselves, we can risk curiosity, wonder, spontaneous delight, or any experience that reveals the human spirit.
—E.E. Cummings, American poet

So what is resiliency? It is how people deal with difficult events that change their lives. It could be the loss of a job, a death of a loved one, serious illness, terrorist attacks, divorce, or other traumatic experiences. With all of these events, many people react to such circumstances with a flood of emotions, and more importantly, a sense of uncertainty.

The American Psychological Association (APA) in 2011 produced a paper called the "Road to Resilience." And it aligns nicely with the context of this section so I will reference it and provide my own interpretations and questions for you to consider throughout this section.

Being resilient is ordinary, not extraordinary, and available to us any time. This doesn't mean one won't experience pain or stress, and it's not a trait you can either have or not. It involves behavior, thoughts, and actions that can be learned or developed in anyone. When you combine behavior, thoughts, and actions with strong relationships that help to create safety, support, trust, and love, it is a powerful foundation to build your resiliency muscle on. Add encouragement and guidance and it is an automatic resiliency booster. There is optimism, hope, and possibilities for us to look forward to in the immediate and near future.

So where you can take responsibility and action begins with a positive self-reflection and self-confidence that you have the strength, ability, and personal free will to change the situation. "How?" you ask.

1. Do a quick assessment of where you are being triggered, and what value or need is it challenging?

2. Decide on an action plan that is realistic and take steps (even small ones matter) in the direction of the desired change.
3. Use your human capacity to tap into your Emotional Intelligence, gauge your strong feelings and reactions, and how you can take control of the choice(s) you want to make regarding the situation or relationship at hand.
4. Take advantage of your problem-solving skills along with effective communications to work through the situation in the most detached way possible.

TIP: One of the tricks I used when in corporate America was when there was conflict and emotional attachment, in the moment I learned to pause, reframe, and then detach and see the person or situation as if it was my largest client ... and decided to act out accordingly versus totally emotionally.

Eleven Ways to Build Resilience

Friendship with oneself is all important, because without it you cannot be friends with anyone else in the world.
—Eleanor Roosevelt, American first lady

Connections, community, and collaboration with others build your social support and can help you to reclaim your hope and courage; and to help others in a time of need, ultimately strengthening you along the way. What gets you out of your head? Think about a time when you were supporting someone through a challenge. How did you feel during the process? Were you happy that they asked for help and accepted it? This is the gift of giving and receiving. We as women don't know how to ask for what we want and we discuss this in more details in the section on Negotiation in this chapter.

Eleven Tips for Building Resilience!

1. We can't always change a crisis or a problem but **we can change how we handle it**. Reflect on how the future circumstances may look and visualize the changes you desire. **What we think about comes about!** We can stay in our heads and work this event from a place of negativity, fear, and feeling stuck, or with the ability to move into positive thoughts, feelings, and actions creating what we want instead. Even in the face of adversity, subtle shifts begin to happen and we feel more personal power in the situation. People often respond more favorably to a highly-energized, positive person and want what you have; share it with them.

2. **Accept that change is a part of life**. And when adversity strikes, be willing to let go of the goals that are no longer attainable as a result of the situation. There are circumstances we cannot change: accept them and work with those circumstances you can impact favorably. You can only change how you respond to anything—it's the power of choice. That said, when you are in the moment and not feeling in total control of your emotions, trust you are doing the best you can in that moment. There are other moments to make different choices, and that is your personal free will to do so.

3. **Forward movement shifts our energy fields**. Set realistic goals and do something on a regular basis to create new patterns, habits, and beliefs—even if they seem small they are still relevant. Focus on your accomplishments instead of focusing on tasks that seem unachievable. Ask yourself:

> *What one thing can I accomplish today that helps me move into the direction I want to go?*
> *What are the steps I need to make in order to begin moving?*
> *What are three things that I can easily do right now to make it feel more manageable?*
> *Who else can I ask for assistance with this situation?*

4. **Take decisive actions.** Act on adversity and adverse situations instead of detaching completely hoping it will go away. It's okay to step into your fear, uncertainty, and doubt, for these are emotions—not things that can hurt you. You have the ability to reframe any situation at any time. Remember the 90-second rule around the emotion of fear—if you count to ninety and let it go, fear will subside. It can then be reframed at any time so it doesn't hurt you.

5. **Look for opportunities of self-discovery**; they are the gifts we received as a result of struggles or loss. Self-discovery is a lifelong journey of empowerment, growth, and expansion. You cannot be stopped when you are being your authentic and powerful self. Always look for opportunities to learn something about your choices, reactions, and feelings and reflections on what you learned as a result of a given situation.

6. Most of us who experience hardship have reported better relationships and a greater sense of strength, even while feeling vulnerable, with an increased sense of self-worth and a heightened appreciation for life. (This is me!) And I take the opportunity every day to **be grateful for all the adversity and challenges** that ultimately create opportunity and endless possibilities in my life. Let me add that there are still moments that the intention to feel grateful is there, yet there are times when something strikes at the emotional

chord deep down and conjures up old negative feelings and we act out from them. We are human, after all, and can only do the best we can in the moment with the power to change it in the next moment(s).

7. **Take time to nurture a positive view of self.** Develop confidence in your ability to solve problems; trusting intuition/instincts helps build resilience. **What we think about comes about.** Choose your thoughts, feelings, and actions in a positive way.

> *When was the last time you did something that made you feel proud and positive?*
> *How did you keep those feelings going?*
> *What example can you remember when you felt that there was nothing that could stop you?*

Keep these memories fresh in your mind in order to access them when you need them.

8. **Keep things in perspective.** Even when facing difficult times try and put the situation in a broader context, keeping a long-term perspective, and minimize blowing the situation out of proportion. This is very difficult in the heat of the situation, and we let our heads manipulate the event or circumstances—defaulting to old patterns or unconscious reactions. We can control this moment with awareness and insight of our limited beliefs and default patterns, and have the personal will to change them anytime we want even when at times that seems impossible.

9. **Expect good things will happen in your life**, visualize what you want rather than worry and feel (emotions not facts). Keeping a hopeful attitude and an optimistic outlook puts you in a place of positive energy. We are in charge of our emotions most of the time, and those times when we aren't

CHAPTER THREE: AUTHENTICITY

it's a matter of awareness, intention, attention, and action toward a different behavior or pattern in the face of adversity.

10. **Take care of yourself**; pay attention to your needs and feelings and engage in activities you enjoy. Take time to relax, exercise, and walk in nature to refresh and rejuvenate. If you have been on an airplane you've heard the flight attendant say, "Put your oxygen mask on first before assisting others," because if you aren't able to take care of yourself you cannot assist others with success.

11. **Learn something new, build connections and bonds, and restore hope** by meditation or spiritual practices that move you into inspired action. Whatever methodology brings you into a space of peace, ease, and grace—tap into it. It could be walking, listening to music, or bird watching. It doesn't matter what you do as long as it activates a calming effect. Building relationships helps you in every facet of your life. There are all types of relationships to build into your life.

The APA offers up a good summary: "On a river, you may encounter rapids, turns, slow water and shallows. As in life, the changes you experience affect you differently along the way. In traveling the river, it helps to have knowledge about it and its past experience in dealing with it."

Your journey should be guided by a plan, a strategy you consider likely to work for you. The rudder is like your inner guidepost helping you navigate what is seen and unseen with intuition, and trusting the process along with your natural skills, abilities, and emotional intelligence.

I talked about hitting the glass ceiling while in corporate America, yet we have an inner glass ceiling that is equally disempowering and sometimes tougher to deal with. The glass ceilings in work are fairly transparent if you are open to see them. But the inner glass ceilings are those often unconscious limited beliefs such as: "not good enough," "smart enough," "pretty enough," or "worthy enough." These are disempowerment patterns that keep us playing small.

Yet once we are aware of the limited self-talk messages being said that's when resilience kicks in! Our inner guide/intuition gets loud enough to finally listen, and brings us into inspired action. In order to break through these patterns, we need to listen and trust the subtle messages that move us forward in a positive way. Facing adversity with passion and purpose help our breakdowns to become breakthroughs that are constantly building our resilience muscle.

TIP: You have the power to recreate any situation that is not working for you, and that includes making the tough choices on whether you are a victim or a victor! You stay or you go! Say yes to what you want and no to what you don't! It is your personal power to decide how your life is being shaped by you and not for you. Practice when a situation presents itself.

Chapter Four

Alliances/ Common-Unity

The forces of a powerful ally can be useful and good to those who have recourse to them ... but are perilous to those who become dependent on them.
—Niccolo Machiavelli, Italian historian

Who do you know, who knows you, what do they know about you, and why do they want to know you? How do you establish a rapport and leverage these alliances for something bigger than yourself? Think about what you're passionate about and how you can be more in alignment with it. It starts with your "community"!

Community

There can be no vulnerability without risk; there can be no community without vulnerability; there can be no peace, and ultimately no life, without community.
—M. Scott Peck, American author and psychiatrist

When you think of community what comes up for you?

My definition for community is "common-unity," where a group of people share similar intentions, beliefs, resources, needs, risks, and passion for something bigger than themselves. For example, you have those who are diehard Apple users, or Rolling Stones groupies, and of course there is the Harry Potter crowd and *Dancing with the Stars* fans (that would be me). From caveman times up until today, we live and work in groups.

My intention for this section of the book is to share a few "aha" moments around the concept of communities, the importance of them, the vulnerability and risk of community commitment, and how the value of contribution, collaboration, and commitment to make a difference is a huge gift to yourself and others.

For many years I had a professional community where groups of people with the same occupation—and in my case it was sales, marketing, and business development—connected on how we could grow and expand what we did for work. They were both in-person and virtual communities and often collaborated around a conference.

The company I worked for was my "common-unity," where we were all working toward something we had in common, and many times it was a space where creativity and commitment played a big role in the success factor. We shared our passion and purpose for being connected around the similar goals and desired outcomes for the short- and long-term. Many of the people I worked with became my "working family," where strong bonds created friendships and business relationships that fostered a sense of belonging.

Most people have several active communities at any given time, and we stay in them because it is comfortable, what we know, and easy not to create change. I would ask you to take a few minutes and assess the communities you belong to and what you gain personally from being a member.

CHAPTER FOUR: ALLIANCES/COMMON-UNITY

> *How would you like to see it help you more?*
> *Is it an environment where you're respected, valued, understood, and heard?*
> *Does the community fuel your passion and purpose?*

If you answered "yes" to these questions then congratulations to you. And if you answered "no," there is some work to be done, or shifting of your time and commitment, somewhere else.

On and in my lifelong journey, personal development at all levels has been a passion and purpose, and I find myself expanding many community circles based on my needs at any given time. I have my professional community, where the focus is all about helping to advance women, and especially equality around pay and advancing positions in the ranks and the boardrooms.

Then there are the communities specific to my development needs at any specific time. Spiritual development has been at the core of my deeper work: seeking meaning in my life and how to help others find meaning too.

My prosperity and abundance communities (see the Law of Attraction and BraveHeart Women later in this chapter), create the opportunity for me to see something new and different about my limited beliefs and how to shift them in a more positive and meaningful way. When you are in a room of people all desiring something similar, it is very energizing and purposeful. We discuss the possibilities and experience tools and techniques to make the shifts we want.

And then there is the family community, which may not consist of like-minded people, yet they provide support, safety, and love when you need it, and they challenge you when you need that too. What I find most interesting about the family circles is just how much the past dictates the future. How the stories of the past are who you are to them. Not who you are today, or how you have evolved and grown, but what they choose to remember and label you from the past. There will be the opportunity to test, stretch, use your voice, silence your voice, practice patience and timing techniques, and most of all, the continued validation that love is the strongest link. Forgiveness and understanding will be practiced here in a safe and worthwhile way. This is a huge opportunity for you to practice all of the new learning of human spirit and dynamics where it matters most to you.

Self-Help for Everything!

Your mind knows only some things. Your inner voice, your instincts, knows everything. If you listen to what you know instinctively, it will always lead you down the right path.
—Henry Winkler, actor

It was after the 9/11 attack that I felt drawn more toward the spiritual side of my personal development journey. I had to find the answers to the burning questions that were consuming my mind, and without release and movement I thought I would remain stuck in fear. Our safety and security were taken from us and the fear of when it was going to happen again lurked in the air.

I always have been able to go into the place of fear, but never had the ability to stay there. All my life I was seeking and finding a different and more positive way to live my life on purpose. Although I was doing this unconsciously at the time, it has been at the core of my belief system forever. I have learned to honor the uncertainty and look for the gifts it is providing.

Seeking answers to the questions such as, "How do I feel safe again?" and "I am creating a new life as a single person, what does this really mean?" And more importantly, "How can I be a strong female influence and mother for my daughter, Jamie?" With all the uncertainty in our personal lives and the world around us we must remain aware and choose to be the advocate for personal power.

CHAPTER FOUR: ALLIANCES/COMMON-UNITY

So after 9/11, I was curious and trusting that there was something bigger than my logic and conscious thought, I started to follow what I call the "universal" breadcrumbs that led me to where I needed to go. I have been an avid student of endless possibilities and found myself attracting like-minded people and groups into my life.

Basically anything you need or think you need is out there under the umbrella of the self-help market, and it is a $13 billion market and growing larger every year. When I felt stuck and wondered *Is this all there is?* I began to notice all the resources, workshops, seminars, books (and the list goes on), that were available. Mind you they had been there all along, but I didn't know what I was looking for until I consciously asked the question. *What am I meant to discover here today?* You heard me say many times through the book: **We don't know what we don't know until we know it**, and only then can we choose.

The more I questioned or was curious about something, the more information was at my fingertips, providing just the right message at the right time. I checked in with my intuitive self and asked, "Is this right for me?" When the answer felt like a strong "yes," I confidently moved into the commitment to seek more.

My experiences have been nothing short of amazing in most cases, and I will share some of them with you. Of course, there is a dark side of this self-help industry, and I say this not to discourage, but to plant a seed of caution as you move on your journey. Remember we talked about the Law of Polarity: Everything has an opposite side to it, such as yes/no or right/wrong.

Let's face it, when we are seeking or searching for answers to the conscious questions or the unconscious unrest we are feeling, we want answers. We are feeling vulnerable, and like most people, we assume external forces will give us the answers or solutions, right? Yes, I have found that the external forces activate the awakening process and many times give me those powerful "aha" moments that move me forward on my path. I admit having many déjà vu moments feeling like, "This information is so familiar to me, and it feels like validation for how far I have come and gives me the confidence to keep seeking."

We tend to gravitate to the gurus, experts, and master teachers that have passion, purpose, and unwavering belief in everything they say and do. All or most have good intentions on sharing what they know, and charging for what they know, all with the desire to help others, right?

Personally I was drawn to many "teachers" that activated my curiosity and strong desire to know more, and I dived right in a big and expensive way because I did not know what I did not know, and even if I did, at some level something was calling me more into action. Each of these experiences has enriched my life and deepened my understanding of me and the belief of endless possibilities we all have in life.

I share a few examples of this only for the purpose of creating awareness of what is out there and to bring it to the conscious mind for the reader.

First, is the example I talked about on vision boards in Chapter Three when I went to Capri, Italy, for a twelve-day program; unsure of why and what I was signing up for. It was a sign; it was something that felt right and I said yes. On the flight over, my fear, doubt, and uncertainty kicked in and my logical mind was screaming: *Are you out of your mind?* It was a big decision, a long trip, and a very expensive commitment financially.

I did not know anyone or even what to expect! I got there and the hotel was exactly the one I had on my vision board. *Okay, this must be right.* Then I walked into a room of thirty other people (all of these people spent this kind of money to be here), *so it must be worth it.* Interestingly enough, I was one of a few Americans attending … hmm! The short version was that at my gut level a doubt about the "guru" was immediate. "And now what?" I asked myself. I just made a huge financial and time commitment and the guy was a flake! I wanted to run, but that was not going to be so easy.

CHAPTER FOUR: ALLIANCES/COMMON-UNITY

That night I really had to work on my mindset and reframe what I wanted to get out of my time there, regardless of my feelings about this man. I was able to shift and open up to learn what I was meant to learn coming from the place of curiosity. I did not buy into some of the stuff he was professing, yet there were things he shared that were new and interesting that I could embrace. Fast forward; it was one of the most amazing experiences of my life—I still use the tools today, and it opened and cleared me up of many limited beliefs that were holding me back from my personal power.

The second experience I will share created a profound shift in me and a validation that indeed all the power we need and require when we need it already resides inside if we stop to listen to our inner voice. I was searching the web when this seminar popped up that was going to be in San Francisco, and it was free. I am good with free so I signed up and went.

Okay, let me say this guru had me at hello! I loved what he had to say and felt the calling to commit to an upcoming weekend program. I brought a friend for the two-for-one offer and it was intense, deep, and demanding with some heavy selling on the entire "life-enhancing" program that would take you deeper and deeper on your spiritual journey. "No, I am not signing up for anything," I thought, and I repeated it out loud to my friend, and then found myself at the table signing up for everything. I don't believe it was a conscious decision, yet I was deeply moved to say yes—it felt right, and I was once again committing a lot of money to find what I was looking for!

Briefly, each of the workshops did provide new and interesting insight along with high-risk, trust-me exercises that had been "proven" to work because this guru said so. I experienced walking on hot coals, breaking boards with my hand, and did a free fall from a high ledge into people's arms trusting they would catch me (this did not go so well), to name a few. I participated in many of them and others I refused because my inner voice was screaming, "Run. Run now while you can!" What happens when you are in a group of people all saying "yes" and you want to say "no"? Do you go along with the crowd or stand firm in your convictions?

I said yes and bought into a series of workshops and attended several of them, and soon realized a sense of doubt and an obvious change in how the "guru" was increasingly riskier and riskier in his practice and expectations. My flag was up, and I cautiously continued on the journey with this community of wonderful people I got to meet.

During one of the sessions, my alarm bells were ringing: "It is time to be done here, Carole, you have learned what you came here to learn now move on!" I sat with this deep, inner voice urging me to go and realized I had learned what I needed to know at this time and place in my life. I decided not to complete the remaining workshops and felt very good about the decision. All of the wisdom, insight, and knowledge I did get from his workshops helped to make the decision to honor my inner voice, express gratitude for the experiences, and more importantly, embrace the newer, stronger, and powerful woman I was becoming in the world with grace and ease.

When we are seeking, we are vulnerable; there is no doubt about it. We are looking for answers or change to something that is not working out for us. We put our belief and trust in someone else's hands and hope that they will pull us through, and most times this works. (This is not just in the self-help industry—I am talking about relationships we cultivate as well.)

We gravitate to the "masters" or "experts" in the areas we need most at the time. We are seeking because we feel lost, unclear, and dissatisfied, and a subtle and sometimes strong desire to know what more we could be doing in our lives. We are all "masters" and an expert of our lives. There is the "10,000-hour rule" that Malcolm Gladwell repeats continually in his book *Outliers: The Story of Success*. I'll summarize that it's a matter of practice in a specific area for a total of 10,000 hours, which allows a person to have a unique, proprietary perspective on the niche or subject. This highly-valuable expertise allows a person to become truly an "expert."

CHAPTER FOUR: ALLIANCES/COMMON-UNITY

Do you feel like a master? An expert? If not, let's take a look at the other side of it.

Vulnerability

> *Vulnerability is the core, the heart, the center of meaningful human experiences.*
> —Brené Brown, author

Let's touch on vulnerability for a moment. Up until a few years ago I could not even say the word "vulnerability," it would get stuck in my throat! To me, being or feeling vulnerable was a sign of weakness or lack of knowledge. It raised the fear of uncertainty (which was not a problem once I worked through my left brain, right brain, no brain, whole brain process—more on this in "The Brain in Mind" in Chapter Two), and I was not going to show this to very many people, if anyone. Feeling vulnerable kept me seeking and still to this day, wanting to know as much about something of interest as possible. I am always a student first.

If you want to really dig into vulnerability, check out Brené Brown's book *Daring Greatly* and her TEDTalk episodes on the subject. Vulnerability is a scary yet powerful and authentic way to live.

When I heard Brené Brown's TEDTalk a few years ago it struck me at the core and moved me toward digging deeper about my own vulnerability and how to own it versus avoiding it at all costs. She says that "... vulnerability is the birth place of love, belonging, joy, courage, empathy, and creativity. It's the source of hope, empathy, accountability, and authenticity. If we want greater clarity, in our purpose or deeper meaningful spiritual lives, vulnerability is the path."

This resonated with me and it was like giving me permission to be okay with vulnerability. It's interesting that since I have allowed myself to be in this space more often than ever before the results from the inside out have been tremendous. I feel my relationships are deeper and more meaningful as a result of this too.

> *Embracing our vulnerabilities is risky but not nearly as dangerous as giving up on love and belonging and joy—the experiences that make us the most vulnerable. Only when we are brave enough to explore the darkness will we discover the infinite power of our light.*
> —Brené Brown, author

Communities Come In All Flavors

> *I look to the future, because that's where I'm going to spend the rest of my life.*
> —George Burns, actor

Mentally, I knew my corporate days were nearing the end and I was preparing to make this big move into the unknown world of entrepreneurship. I remember it was Christmas week, 2005, and my daughter was spending time with her dad. I had a strong urge to walk into an Arthur Murray Dance studio and inquire about any specials they might have that week. (By the way, there are always specials available for most everything you are interested in if you just ask.)

All my life I was inspired by dancers, and especially ballroom dancing. I would sit for hours watching the dance competitions on PBS back in the day and just loved the elegance and grace of the dancers. Arthur Murray had a program for five private lessons and one group dance party for under $200.00, and I signed up.

My first lesson was the swing dance and I loved it, it was natural and relatively easy (or so I thought at the time), since I danced the swing with my dad growing up. I was hooked immediately and found myself buying a package and joining the Arthur Murray

CHAPTER FOUR: ALLIANCES/COMMON-UNITY

Dance community. And six weeks later I was participating in a dance showcase and four weeks after that in a regional competition—what? Something creative awakened in me and it was opening up parts of me I didn't even know existed. Especially dressing up in glamorous gowns, and slightly revealing Latin style dresses, the makeup and hair, and becoming a total feminine being while in that space.

The dancing community is a very tight-knit group and much more magical than I expected, yet it is still an industry that makes money. Dancing is not an inexpensive hobby, and it requires full commitment and dedication if you want to excel up in the ranks. Let me say that dancing is MUCH harder than it looks and it requires focus, determination, passion, and purpose in order to be good, let alone great. Being a competitive person I wanted to get there as fast as I could because that level of dancing was so much more involved!

Through this process I learned how to really hear music for the first time. I could actually count the beats, hear the words, and feel the movement in my body. It helped me get in touch with me; much like yoga and meditation does for others. I was able to express my creativity and feelings through movement—the dance, and ultimately the dance of life.

Dancing with the Stars was doing a thirty-city tour the first year I was dancing, and they were looking for local amateur dancers to open up the show with a dance off for the crowd—to let the world know anyone can dance. We had to try out. It was 2006, exactly one year to the date I started dancing, and I got picked as one of the candidates. It was held at the HP Pavilion (now called the SAP Center) in San Jose, California in front of thousands of people. We had no instructions on what dance or who we would be partnered with, just to be ready when they called us! *What?* I was feeling fear and wondering to myself, "What the heck are you thinking, Carole?" Fortunately, I was matched up with a wonderful man who also danced at our studio and he was fun, roughly the same age, and his motivation for dancing was to prepare for his daughter's wedding. We laughed at what we were about to do and agreed to just have fun, and we did.

My thirty seconds of fame landed my picture on the front page of the *San Jose Mercury News* website alongside an interview. We were the only couple to be interviewed by the reporter, and out of curiosity I asked what made him pick us. "Look around, there are young professional dancers dressed to impress like the pros from the show. When I spotted the two of you practicing, it was clear you were there to have fun and would make headline news," he said. "You two are an inspiration at any age." He did ask our age, and proudly we shared, and then I asked him not to post it in the article with a smile. It was a turning point in my life, and I continued dancing—making it to an advanced level until I made the move back to Boston. I so appreciated all of the delightful surprises dancing revealed, and more importantly, how meaningful it was to my self-discovery.

BraveHeart Women

> *The woman's mission is not to enhance the masculine spirit, but to express the feminine; hers is not to preserve a man-made world, but create a human world by the infusion of the feminine element into all of its activities.*
> —Margaret Thatcher, former British prime minister

Dancing opened up my feminine side when I did not have any real awareness that it existed. The rules of business had been created by men, who by nature have more of the masculine energy. As I continued to evolve I wanted to learn more about what makes us different by gender and how I could show up more in my natural state of being. I found myself more approachable, less stressed, and willing to let go of being in total control (or so I thought).

CHAPTER FOUR: ALLIANCES/COMMON-UNITY

I was finally open to be in another relationship after the many years of being single again. And sure enough, the absolute best person showed up in my life at the time I released the old to make room for the new. Tapping into my feminine side was and continues to be a process that is evolving all the time.

Aligning femininity with my purpose to help with the advancement of women (and a few good men) made it clear that talking about this was important. *But wait, I need to know more and seek others to teach me all about it since I don't know anything!* See a cycle here? We are always seeking from others what we don't believe or trust we know already.

I was told I was a "brave heart woman" and thought to myself, "If there is not a community out there, maybe I will start one," and sure enough, I went online and found the BraveHeart Women site. I so resonated with their vision, mission, and purpose—why would I need to start my own? I could join in and collaborate with this massive movement that aligned with me!

I signed up to the member site first and found the messaging and the power of "tribe" to welcome me in and support my journey. I took the next leap and went to their four-day conference. Imagine walking into a room of 700-plus women with an energy level that could move the building. This was my first experience of being in a 100-percent, women-only forum and it was amazing. There were women connecting soul-to-soul and heart-to-heart from all over the globe and it was very moving for me. I had an internal dialog going on to remind me not to say yes to any new programs they would be selling, and to remember my past experiences in order not to repeat.

My emotions overruled my logic, and as a master at justifying anything, I did so once again. I signed up for a four-day retreat for January in Arizona (dead of winter on the East Coast), called the Feminine Success Model. Once again, not knowing what to expect I went with an open mind and open heart to learn what I was meant to learn.

A long story short—the experience was amazing, deep, and definitely brought me tremendous insight to what was continuing to hold me back. I learned more about Divine Feminine and Divine Masculine energy and how both needed to be in play for harmony in our lives (the Universal Law of Correspondence).

The essence of the Divine Feminine is the spark of life when everything is connected and in the flow. Energy that grows our plants also grows us. It is the innate body, heart, gut, and wisdom that all human beings have within them. It's our ability to sense, feel, and intuit our highest options. Divine Feminine traits include empathy, consciousness, connection, belonging, meaning, purpose, and contribution, to name a few.

Understanding the importance and value of the feminine aspects and the awakened Divine Masculine in us is our ability to be aware of and acknowledge what we know from our experiences, rather than from what we are told. This opens us up new and exciting channels to explore. Divine Masculine traits include direction, movement, strength, focus, abundance, and clarity to move into action, and why it is so important to embrace these as we move into our personal power.

I have found a "mastermind" group within this community. There is a circle of women that continue to collaborate in helping each other grow their businesses, help them get unstuck, and serve as a sounding board when issues come up—whether it be in business or life. There is definitely a give and take, and amazingly one person's issue can open up something in us at the time between one another. One of the ladies called me regarding a new business idea that she was so excited about and wanted to share it with me. Using the CLARITY techniques I referenced in the "CLARITY" section in Chapter Three, we went through the process and helped her with a new mission statement and roadmap for moving from concept to delivery with more clarity and purpose.

CHAPTER FOUR: ALLIANCES/COMMON-UNITY

Social Communities

With the power of social media and the Internet it just takes a cause, a passion, or a purpose to get a movement in motion. Community involvement is a way to help to build your A-Game in work and life. The people we connect with are a reflection of us and mirror in life what we need or want to see, hear, and remember. How and who you associate with adds to your "brand" in how people see, hear, and remember you.

A community can be two people or two million! And communities can help us explore new ideas, validate what we already know, stretch us out of our comfort zones that are "safe" environments as well as connect, create, and collaborate with others. It is a place where you are aligned with purpose even if you don't know exactly what your purpose is today. If it feels good, easy and in the flow, it is likely on purpose. When resistance happens, this is your inner voice asking you to pause, reflect, and then make a choice.

I continue to find "community" in all areas of my life that provides a space for me to create more self-awareness, bring more of my authentic self to the world, and be heard by using my voice while creating opportunities to develop deeper passion, purpose, and meaning in my life. Connections create relationships that are built on the foundation of likeness, trust, resilience, and "vulnerability that is the core, the heart, the center of meaningful human experiences," as taken from Brené Brown. It is a safe place to stretch, grow, and expand in alliance with passion and purpose.

Ask yourself these questions:

> *I love it when …?*
> *I get fired up when …?*
> *I can't wait until I get …?*
> *I feel alive when …?*
> *I wish every day I can experience …?*
> *I am happiest when …?*

So if you can't find what you want, create it ... you will open up the doors for others to join, follow, and collaborate around a cause or a strong belief so others become aware of it and how it can impact even more people.

Follow your intuition and heart and see where it leads, keep your head on your shoulders, and trust you have the answers within. Trusting that is an avenue toward awakening what is already inside you. Know that there are experts and masters everywhere, just as you are the master of you wherever you go!

TIP: Take time to check in with your feelings and listen to your body. What is it telling you? Feel grace and ease? It's a good sign. Feel tense and stuck? It's time to dig deeper for answers to any meaningful decision. It's a step in the process in creating your life path.

Do not seek to follow in the footsteps of the wise.
Seek what they sought.
—Basho Matsuo, Japanese poet

Chapter Five

Affluence

The world will be saved by the western woman.
—Dalai Lama, Buddhist leader

The intention of this chapter is to shine light on opportunities that may align with your personal passions and desires on how you build your A-Game for the world to experience. There has never been a better time in the world for women to expand their financial footprint and go after what they want to create for themselves. There are thousands of books, articles, and plenty of research on the economy, women's leadership issues, and gender equality, and I will list some of them in the resource section of the book. This chapter is about creating awareness and snapshots of areas that you can leverage today, whether inside an organization or as an entrepreneur, with influence and impact.

Economy

Across the globe, women are the biggest emerging market in the history of the planet—more than twice the size of India and China combined.
—Indra Nooyi, CEO of PepsiCo

There is a tremendous amount of coverage in the media, and a greater amount of research that discusses how it's a great time to be a woman in the world. Yet there is a significant disconnect between who the consumers are and how they base their purchasing decisions. There is a huge dissatisfaction amongst women who find that most marketers are ignoring them, the largest consumer base in the world.

And it's a great time for organizations—and the people that lead these companies and make product decisions, which happens to be predominately men—to change the dynamic in how to reach and respond to the female consumer more effectively.

According the Boston Consulting Group (BCG), the power of the female market will reach $5 trillion in incremental spending in the next five years. It is the time for organizations to connect and capitalize on this by doing more research on the female consumer base and understand how women buy goods and services differently.

How does each gender differ?

If men liked shopping, they would call it research.
—unknown

Men are reluctant store shoppers and much more focused on shopping with intent for a specific item that gets them in and out quickly. With online shopping, men search by product and women search by brand. Men spend more on food, electronics, and entertainment purchases. A few other points: Men have a handle on cash flow, regularly pay bills on time, have general knowledge of stocks, bonds and mutual funds, and are confident in their investment portfolios.

Women buy goods and services based on the emotional benefits: does it make her feel smart, savvy, wise, safe? *I love this new efficient and quiet dryer that has a safety alarm when the lint bin is full.* Her purchase supports all these feelings of money well spent, while men tend to buy based on routine, replacement, durability,

CHAPTER FIVE: AFFLUENCE

and price. *Do I take these shoes to the cobbler's and get them resoled or just buy a new pair?* They want to solve a problem by fixing the shoes versus going to the store and getting a new pair, and by the way, when they do go to the store and buy a new pair, they wondered why they didn't think of that at first!

TIP: Take a few minutes to think about your recent purchases and why you made them. Did they totally meet your expectations? If so, why? If not, why did you settle? We will begin to notice this more just by asking the questions.

Women are challenged with time and balance issues both at work and in life. Men are too, but it does not affect their buying habits, and 73% of any given household's total budget is managed by women. This translates into over $5 trillion in discretionary spending. When women like something, they tell their friends and stimulate the economy and demand for products that will indeed meet the emotion quotient. If a product doesn't meet your expectation, the chances are it won't do well in the sales figures. You have the opportunity to create the ideal marketplace, now is the time to vote with your wallet.

TIP: Try only purchasing from conscious-driven organizations that relate to you and deliver the products you want.

Women are keenly aware of the importance of a sense of community; something that is lacking in most male-developed products. Personal connection is critical, especially in key market areas such as the financial industry and healthcare, where most women feel disregarded and disrespected. Men are still the de facto consumer in these critical areas that are changing the economic landscape now. Next time you are seeking out a service, do your research on what the core values are, how they serve the community, and what is the landscape in the executive suite. The Cataylst 2012 Census study shows virtually no change from 2011 in female leadership roles at Fortune 500 companies. Twenty-seven percent of Fortune 500 companies have NO women on their board—and of the companies that do, only 14.3% of key leadership positions are held by women. An example of this is the popular cable network The Discovery Channel—its parent company Discovery Communications also lists the Oprah Winfrey Network as a channel—have no women on the board! If there are no women on the boards, there is no balance in the decision-making process, and these companies are only serving half the market.

We all have been impacted by the last recession and it has created a turning point in the labor landscape. Men were hurt worse than women, with an 82% job loss held by men, according to *The New York Times*, especially in areas such as construction and manufacturing. Whereas women were employed in areas such as education and nursing, where there is a consistent demand for workers. As a result, women have become the majority of the labor force for the first time in history.

Sadly, this recession is still hitting men the hardest, and it is up to the female energy to collaborate with the masculine energy for a win/win/win outcome. This will be a huge emotional shift in our society that will require patience, support, and alliance across the board in order to bring sustainable balance into our lives and economy. As the job market evolves, it will be in areas that have been predominately supported by women, and now more and more men will be seeking these roles as well. Research indicates that more men are happy to be involved with the family unit as stay-at-home dads and are embracing the experience of their partner being the primary breadwinner (as long as the relationship maintains a level of respect and does not incur an unbalanced dominance).

CHAPTER FIVE: AFFLUENCE

Women business owners are the fastest-growing segment in our economy, and according to 2010 US Census data, of the 76.5% women-founded businesses, 72% of these female business owners never had owned a business before. It's an economic boom that is being recognized in Washington. And the Small Business Association (SBA) loans over 5.7 billion dollars in funding to women-owned businesses with the help from the Recovery Act and the Small Business Jobs Act of 2010 to support this. There are monies and resources supporting women who want to make a difference by following their passion and purpose and stimulating economic growth as a result. Never in our history has there been such support and encouragement for women to step up and out to create their desired outcome.

And this trend speaks to the talent pipeline in many organizations across the globe. Specifically women have been opting out of the workforce at a time when organizations are seeking to fill the executive levels with more diversity in regards to thinking and decision making. Many organizations are faced with the challenge to keep women in the workforce when they choose to have a family. Several organizations are creating options such as on/off ramps to keep employees engaged with the organizations during this phase of their career as a way to resume their careers when ready. This is one of the ways of finding a more balanced way to build business and career opportunities for the changing economy. Many women are discouraged by the lack of role models at the top, do not feel there is real opportunity, and more so, have no desire to keep fighting the boys' club and the unconscious biases that remain.

It still begs the question why so many organizations are leaving money on the table by failing to hire, develop, and promote women to senior-level roles. Catalyst Research shows that organizations that have women in senior-level positions are more profitable, offer greater shareholder value, and maintain a competitive advantage in the marketplace.

So why have we been staying in place for the past twenty years with all the discussion and focus on gender equality? There are so many reasons that it would take several books to cover them in detail. Here, I will explore key factors as a way of creating awareness and to offer a gentle reminder that we all have and make choices in all of our actions. Yes, there are limitations placed on us every day, and we may not want to pave the way for others, yet it is up to you to pave your way toward your desired outcome in work and life. And as a result, you are modeling change and others will see a path toward possibilities for them.

As I mentioned earlier in the book, I didn't even know there was a gender divide and unconscious biases that continued to sabotage me along the way until I got to the pain point in my career and needed to make a change. It was a time to use my left-brain thinking (analysis of the situation and opportunity and preparedness) and my right-brain thinking (the big picture and long-term possibilities that made me happy), along with no-brain thinking (doing nothing until the timing was right), and whole-brain thinking (taking intentional and aspired action for meaningful change).

I have coached so many professional women over the years that just want to give up and quit, and move to another job to only face the same dilemma over and over again. We tend to repeat the same behaviors expecting different results. As you know by reading this book, that change starts and ends with you and for you. Others may want to have a say, but at the end of the day, you have the power of choice.

Savvy Women Lead with Their Voices!

The future belongs to those of us—female or male—who can adopt and embrace the feminine archetype.
—John Hagel III, Co-Chair of Deloitte Touche

CHAPTER FIVE: AFFLUENCE

I had the opportunity to interview some powerful women on my radio show and each of them brought a tremendous level of passion and purpose on women's issues in the workplace. They are on a mission to bring awareness through sound research, and to help be the voice for others while bringing gender equality from a discussion to reality.

Joanna Barsh, senior partner at McKinsey & Co, takes the lead on their "Centered Leadership Project" and is the author of *How Remarkable Women Lead*. We had a long discussion about the challenges organizations have with moving women through the pipeline to the next level of leadership and what is getting in the way. She commented, "When senior leaders commit themselves to gender diversity, they really mean it—but in the heat of the moment, deeply entrenched beliefs cause old forms of behavior to resurface. All too often in our experience, executives perceive women as greater risk for senior positions, fail to give women tough feedback that would help them grow or hesitate to offer working mothers opportunities that come with more travel and stress. The majority of women who make it to senior roles have a real desire to lead, and few think they have meaningful support to do so and even fewer think they are in line to move up."

Personally I experienced this several times in my career, and the one with the biggest impact was when I adopted my daughter Jamie back in 1989. I was a top-performing sales leader and on the fast track into more senior-level leadership roles. As soon as the company management learned of the upcoming adoption, they began to look for my replacement, which I happened to hear about from business associates in the marketplace. There was no "adoption policy" in place, and I was expected to show up at work immediately after taking her home from the hospital as the adoption process was beginning.

The pressure that was applied to me as a new working mother was grossly unfair and insensitive. I did go to the president and CEO of the company expressing my awareness of their plans to replace me because I was a new mother! They immediately denied it and decided to address the lack of an "adoption leave" program for the organization.

They kept the pressure on and I decided to leave after three months. My performance was still at goal or above, and my customers were totally supportive of my new role as a mother and sales partner to them. I had strong relationships with my clients and my marketplace making it difficult that the company was not treating me with fairness and dignity. To come to a win/win/win, I offered to leave the organization with a severance package, a letter of recommendation from the president, and health benefits for an extended period. They gladly agreed to my terms and both parties remained professional and gracious well into the future. They also implemented a respectable "adoption" policy that went into immediate effect after I left the company.

There was a perception that I would not be able to keep up the pace in the territory or travel extensively that was "required" for the job, even though my customers totally supported my adoption process. The gender bias was in full motion. I bring this up for a few reasons. You have a voice and need to use it. If you feel you are not being treated with respect and integrity, you need to speak up. If you dismiss your values for the sake of a paycheck, you are the only one who loses short- and long-term. The job does not define who you are—it's your character, word, and values that define you.

The Wall Street Journal partnered with McKinsey & Co for the "Women in the Economy" research project. They found much evidence that supports the business case for gender diversity. Here's what they had to say:

"The magic begins when leaders achieve real diversity of thought," and thinking about getting the best brains to work as leaders and changing the stubborn barriers is imperative to progress forward. Many executives, both men and women, were excited about the opportunities, but also expressed personal disappointment about their own companies' lack of progress. Despite investment, women opted for staff roles, quit, retired, or even settled in. Does this sound

CHAPTER FIVE: AFFLUENCE

familiar to any of you? Hard-won advances to the executive levels were followed by departures. Are you one of them and if so, why did you opt out? Seasoned and caring leaders privately wondered if the barriers were too significant for victory to be declared.

This I relate to personally. I hit the glass wall, glass cliff, and then the glass ceiling during my career in the publishing industry, and knew it was time to go. A *glass cliff* is when you are asked to take on a high-risk opportunity that is ready to go over the cliff, and the company is willing to take a chance on your leadership to see what you can do. If it succeeds, you're in the club, if it fails, you are to blame and gone. That said, each glass-cliff situation included high risks and high rewards, and that was a personal motivator for me. Fortunately, it paid off positively.

A McKinsey & Co survey on "Unlocking The Full Potential of Women" published in April, 2012, identified four barriers to women's advancement: structural obstacles, lifestyle choices, institutional mind-sets, and individual mind-sets. Leadership teams in the survey have been working hard at removing them, addressing the lack of sponsorship (see Chapter Three), limited flexibility, and unconscious biases. The four barriers are:

1. **Structural obstacles.** Although gender diversity is a priority, only half of the employees agreed there is a commitment to the issue. "Seeing is believing," and there are few women at the top, and actions speak louder than words.

> *How would you navigate around this issue?*
> *What action steps can you take to be seen, heard, and remembered in your efforts to break through this potential barrier?*
> *Do you want to do what it takes for self and others to follow?*
> *Are you interested in changing the ratio from a few to many women at the top?*

2. **Lifestyle choices.** About half of the women surveyed said that they were both the primary breadwinners and primary caregivers in their households. Most of the men who were primary breadwinners were not the primary caregivers. Accordingly, women may choose to slow down their careers or shift roles to increase predictability and lessen travel. Some companies have implemented flexible work schedules to accommodate. This is a personal choice and oftentimes difficult to expect the employees to do it all. Here is where women could benefit more from "Reciprocity Matters" in Chapter Three. Tap into your mentor and sponsor opportunities to keep you visible and in the game. Sheryl Sandberg, CIO of Facebook and author of *Lean In* tells us, "Don't quit before you leave," and to plan for what you desire and work your plan.

3. **Institutional mind-sets** used by successful executives being and acting like men, leaders expect women to model the same behavior. In the McKinsey survey one CEO said, "Women don't knock on my door the way men do or ask for advice. I wish they would be more proactive." And when leaders pay attention to the differences, they may respond in ways that limit options for women who can juggle family and work. Here is where assumptions made about others or situations come into play. It is up to you to create your professional brand instead of others creating it for you. Who you know, who knows you, and what do they know about you is imperative in shaping your desired future.

I believe there is a major shift happening in the workplace, and there are many successful stories of women making it to the top by choice. Many of us adapted to the male environments and had to overcome extraordinary challenges through stamina, resilience, and sheer grit—with positive results.

There are limitations placed upon us from time to time, yet

we have the freedom of choice—even if not immediate—a choice to plan with passion and purpose aligning what matters most for you. Even in a job that you may not want long-term, how do you capitalize on the opportunity to meet influential people, develop new skills, and take on the stretch assignments that can expose you to new knowledge and business opportunities? It is up to us to make the best of every situation regardless of the agenda of others. Often we don't feel like we have the choice, but it is always about personal choice.

The "SHE" Change (Sea Change)

Women have earned the reputation of being more secure and patient investors. Female investors were more likely to hold onto assets longer and sell when the time was optimum reducing their losses.
—Faith Popcorn, futurist

Since the 1990s I have been following Faith Popcorn—futurist, author, and internationally-known speaker and expert in market trends, with an accuracy rate of better than 90%. The SHE Change is her latest prediction.

A *sea change* is any widespread sweeping shift that affects all elements of a system. The SHE change is, according to Popcorn's team of researchers, "In the coming decade we will see a sea change in the way feminine power is incorporated in society. Characteristics once thought to be solely the province of women will be adopted as best practices." As you build your A-Game it is important to not only know what you value but to expect to be paid fairly for the value and results you deliver. Women that advance and hone their natural skills through self-awareness, removing limited beliefs, and building a brand presence and authentic voice prepares them for this "SHE change." Popcorn predicts that, "Monetary domination will cease to be the sole metric by which success is measured. Women will put people before profit and won't demand the same exorbitant salaries and bonuses for which male counterparts have been infamous." It is not about competing for more but to expect to get what you deserve and feel good about it.

You are already a master of this next big trend. Popcorn explains, "traditional female behavior will become preferred in business," so bring it forward with confidence and resolve.

We've discussed the critical role Emotional and Social Intelligence in organizations, and Popcorn says, "Companies will value employees of both genders who demonstrate consciousness over extraversion and testosterone decision making," ensuring female focus is maintained. **Be seen, be heard, and be remembered** as your authentic self and you are immediately contributing to change and positive results.

Investing in the New Economy

To achieve the economic expansion we seek, we need to unlock a vital source of growth that can power our economies in decades to come. And that vital source of growth is women.
—Hillary Clinton, politician

Women are closing the gap financially. And women are better investors, according to *Warren Buffet Invests like a Girl*. The book states that female stockbrokers experience a higher return and earn an average of 9%, while the male stockbrokers' return is 5.82%. This prompted me to review my portfolio and who and how it was being managed to ensure I was getting the better return on my investment. The good news is that I am, and the better news is it managed by a man with his female associate—I refer to this as the "gender partnership."

"The SHE change is exactly what society needs right now. We need to rely on compassion more than competition and innovation more than invasion. The introduction of the new feminine power

CHAPTER FIVE: AFFLUENCE

into all aspects of our lives will bring about a new era of productivity and peace," says Popcorn.

What a wonderful time to be a woman in this world. There never has been a better time in our history that empowers women as it does today. Being perfectly imperfect in the process of bringing feminine power to the forefront offers challenge and opportunity, grace and ease, freedom of choice and the ability to **be seen, be heard, and be remembered** in your unique and authentic way. We each have a responsibility to seize this opportunity to create more abundance and wealth for our lives, our country, and the world at large.

TIP: Review your financial portfolio, decide if you are happy with your knowledge, or if you need to learn more. Is the portfolio managed by you or someone else? If others, what is their role and are you ready to handle it if it was up to you? Know what you don't know and seek to find the answers.

Chapter Six

Advocate

It's never too late to think about who you know and what you know. How you advocate for yourself and others is your legacy in motion. Many people think that legacy begins later in life, but realize in hindsight it begins early in life. It does not matter what stage of life you are in, you are contributing to your legacy. This chapter is about creating awareness and encouragement to take the lead in your legacy building.

Legacy

> *Carve your name on hearts, not tombstones. A legacy is etched into the minds of others and in the stories they share about you.*
> —Shannon Alder, author

Inside each of us there is a need and desire to be heard, to have our innermost thoughts, feelings, and desires expressed to others to see, hear, and remember. It doesn't matter what you do as long as you impact real change that moves yourself and others forward in a positive way.

CHAPTER SIX: ADVOCATE

And your story is the greatest legacy you will leave for your family and friends and strangers that will hear and remember your history. So, now you might be thinking, "What story? I am just living life as ordinary people do and what's there to remember?" I dare say plenty! No one comes into this world being ordinary but unique in every way. Everything we do is unique and can't be duplicated. All of the ups and downs and wins and losses have built character, confidence, resilience, and determination in ways that others have not.

We all have a story in us. Even if you don't put pen to paper you are always telling your story by the actions you take every day. Someone always is watching … my question to you is: What do you want them to see, hear, and remember?

I actually only started to think about my legacy a few years ago and this might be the case for you as well. But when I began to think about my daughter, family, and friends that I will one day leave behind, I wondered, "What would they think about me? What would they say about me? And would they wished I had done things differently that could have had a greater impact in the world?"

When I was sharing this with a friend he asked, "What are you talking about…? You have done so much in your life, and overcome so many obstacles, and faced adversity head-on, and you are standing taller than ever—that's part of your legacy. What you do for others day in and day out—that is your gift you give and its part of YOUR legacy. I have never met anyone so interesting and strong, and I don't think I could have handled half the things you have in life—that is your legacy and it got me thinking … what is mine going to look like?"

A fantastic question that took the conversation away from me and on to him through a series of great conversations that followed in the weeks to come. My first reaction to the conversation was it is never too late to create your legacy; it's a matter of reflecting on your life in the past and what you desire to do from this moment on.

What is your legacy?

- ***What do you want people to say about you***—not so much when you are gone, but while you are still alive and with us? How would you describe your greatest attributes in work and in life? Are they different or consistent no matter what? Do they align with your core values and integrity? If you don't like how you handled something did you give up or work toward correcting and changing the outcome?

- ***Are there people in your life that bring the best out in you*** and if so, what are the things you value about these people? Does it mirror what is important to you or does it cause you to want more of what they have? If it's more of what they have, how do you go about integrating it into your life and why? What about the people you don't like, do you know what about them creates this feeling? Is there something about you that you wish to change? What steps will you take to begin this process?

- ***What have you done that you are most proud of and why?*** What are the feelings you have when you remember these times? Are there any common themes that come up and if so, what are they and what about them do you value most? What do you want to be sure to bring more of in your life starting right now? What's it going to take to do it? And if not now, when? What will stop you from fulfilling your desires?

When I asked these questions of myself over the past few years, I found just asking created change. Now that doesn't mean I took full action on everything, but it did create awareness and thoughts, feelings, and potential actions for me to consider. *Maybe today is not right, but ultimately I would like to do xyz.* That is a form of action because I did set an intention that one day xyz would happen.

CHAPTER SIX: ADVOCATE

Every year people create their New Year's resolutions with good intentions and determination to not fall short of meeting or exceeding their goals. Why? Well, I can't answer for everyone, but chances are the goals were lofty, did not follow the SMART goal process, and life got in the way. Life is always going to get in your way; it's a matter of making choices that move you in the direction of your desired outcome—and that is action; even small steps count!

In lieu of the resolution process, I spend time at the end of the year reflecting on what I accomplished and what I failed to accomplish. I go through the emotional dialog, the self-doubt, the jealousy, frustration, and anger towards those who seem to have done what I wanted to do with ease and I enjoy a full-blown pity party all by myself. I release all of the negative emotions and work with the energy-drainer exercise model from Chapter Two to work through each of the major energy drainers—and then decide what I want instead. I list all of the options to make it happen and begin to work on them one step at a time until I accomplish what I set out to do.

TIP: Reflect on the year, journal your thoughts and then review what you wrote. What jumps off the page is where you want to start. Create a manageable-size list knowing that life changes can create change. Leaving room for new things to focus on is important. Apply the SMART rule and consider it a guidepost as you create your life.

I find the reflection process forces me to look at my life here and now and honestly see how much I actually do contribute to the world just by being me. I give myself permission to be honest with my accomplishments without diminishing the value of them (we tend to diminish them as no big deal), and I choose to add new goals and stretch goals that keep me challenged in the right way for the near future. Here's when the good stuff really happens for me. I take a notebook or the computer and just begin to write whatever is on my mind without too much thought or judgment. I don't worry about typos; I just download what is coming up for me. I write until I stop, meaning with no set time or agenda, and only when there is nothing left to write. My experience has been both quick and to the point or long and detailed with emotions, with a clear understanding for what I need to do next. Either way I respect the process. I also believe this process can move you from conscious thought to what I call the "stream of unconsciousness"; and that's where the gems reveal themselves.

Remember I had surgery in 2010 to fix my paralyzed vocal cords and once again woke up with no voice for several weeks that followed. I dealt with every emotion possible from sadness to anger and everything in between. I could have wallowed in my sadness, but I opted to go through this process and see what was revealed to me. And here are a few of the messages that came up loud and clear.

I had a limited voice most of my life and it delivered me more gifts than I ever imagined, and that would not change no matter what the outcome of this surgery was. I knew it was time to share these gifts I received in a much bigger way even though the fear of "not being heard" still plagued me. And it was time to write, speak, and finally be on a radio show that I desired to do for many years.

Thirty years ago someone asked me if I could do anything what would it be and I said, "I want my own talk show on the radio." He laughed and said, "Lofty dream, but you don't have the voice to carry it off," and it always stuck in my mind. And the biggest message from that experience was it is okay to be vulnerable, because without learning how to step into your own power by choice, you will continue living a limited life by choice.

Amazing things happen when awareness, intention, attention, and action are applied to our goals. Shit happens fast! Right after I

CHAPTER SIX: ADVOCATE

finished the exercise of writing down what I wanted, I got a call to coauthor a chapter in a book about transformation, and clearly I had a story. I said yes and a second opportunity to coauthor another book came a few months later. As I shared in Chapter Three, I expressed my fear about being vulnerable with a few people, and each of them had the similar fears. We all realized that we were human and could help each other through these moments. It also shows that when things are in the dark (our heads) they can be as big, ugly, and scary as we want, but when we shine the light on it (talking about it) it is not as bad as the thoughts we created around it.

Last year I hosted a live talk show on Voice America called *The AWE Factor* (Advancing Women Everywhere) and fulfilled my dream to be on the radio. I loved the experience, and more importantly, the connections I made with smart, savvy women who share my passion to make a difference in the world. And lastly, I faced my vulnerability head-on, and even though it was there, it did not have power over me; rather I had the power over it.

And now the real vulnerability test is with this book. This is the book that has been inside of me and meant to come out for several years. I actually found one of my old notebooks and was reading it, and realized I had this book named back in 2005! I talked about what I wanted it to be and had no recall that I ever wrote it. Clearly it was unconscious thoughts coming to the surface, but they didn't stay there until this year. I believe that timing is everything and not always in our control, and I trust the process that when the time is right, things begin to happen with more ease.

So what does this have to do with one's legacy? Everything, and it will be different for each one of us. Your uniqueness and gifts need to be expressed and shared in any format that matters to you. Everything that happens in your life is by design, and how you choose to deal with them is your choice. You are tested, prodded, stretched, challenged, defeated, rewarded, nurtured, supported, loved, guided, and protected—every emotion possible is presented to you as gifts to share with others.

Your confidence, character, credibility, courage, personal power, presence, passion, purpose, resilience, integrity, values, vulnerability, and relationship with self and others is *your* authentic self that shows up in the world.

Advocate for Others!

Words are the voice of the heart.
— Confucius, Chinese philospher

Help others to **be seen, be heard, and be remembered**. When you notice someone doing great work—speak up by acknowledging them and sharing it with others, whether in the work environment, community, or family unit. Acknowledgment is one of the easiest gifts to share with others and a simple gesture that carries a lot of impact.

Advocate for a cause that is important to you and ultimately others in the world. Many of us assume someone else will take care of it. Or worse, we hope that the problem or situation gets resolved without having to do something. Assuming others will speak for us is passing the buck and blame that we are not seeing the change we want in the world. It is up to each of us to use our voice for positive change no matter what.

Advocate and vote with your wallet. If you don't like how a marketing campaign is represented and you find it offensive, don't do business with them. If a company is using deplorable labor situations to produce a product and it goes against your core value, stop buying their products. You can advocate for change by NOT doing business with companies that don't value what you value.

Advocate for our children and their future when it comes to the laws that are being implemented or not, our mother earth, and human decisions that are changing the natural landscape forever. What can you do today to help the children tomorrow? Their voices are not being heard, and I ask you to dig deep into your heart and ask: What can you do for them now to ensure a better tomorrow?

Pay It Forward!

We make a living by what we get. We make a life by what we give.
—Winston Churchill, former British prime minister

I remember back in 2002 when the movie *Pay It Forward* came out. It was about a little boy who wanted to make a difference in the lives of three people and each one of them would pay it forward by making a difference in lives of even more people and before you know it millions of people would be paying it forward with a good deed.

This is the simplest and least expensive way to make massive and immediate change in the world. And you don't need to think much about how because there is a movement already happening, and you just need to choose to get on board or not. The movie was based on Catherine Ryan Hyde's book of the same name. Hyde is the creator of a movement and foundation called the Pay It Forward Foundation (www.payitforwardfoundation.org). You can log on to see how they are helping the global community share simple acts of kindness every day. The simple act of you doing something for someone else and have them do something for another person is the way of paying it forward. Simple acts like a smile, or holding the door open, or letting a driver merge ahead of you on the freeway.

Every year there is a global Pay It Forward Day where communities of people all over the globe take part in the event. People intentionally look to offer a glimmer of hope in a small but meaningful way such as simply taking the "pay it forward" bracelet off and giving it to another for them to pass it along yet again. This movement can and should impact our world every single day. This single event is a way of marketing and moving others into action on a much bigger scale.

TIP: Notice, acknowledge, and share in "acts of kindness" by being present to see someone holding the door for another. Stop and say, "That was thoughtful." Or when in the checkout line in a supermarket and you see a mom with children in tow, offer to let her go ahead of you and assist in putting her groceries on the counter. The next time you are in line buying coffee and you see someone in the military, buy them their drink and thank them for their service to our country. The list is endless—just take the first step to notice, and you will bring many smiles to the faces you touch.

There are people in the world that naturally notice, acknowledge, and engage with others by being curious enough to see their name tag and ask them their story. Just by calling someone by their name is an act of kindness. My friend Jack ALWAYS engages with people—whether it is in a store, gas station, restaurant, or anywhere. He makes sure he gets the person's name, addresses them by their name, and asks a question or two about them. A simple act of acknowledgment shifts the energy in a positive way.

The Pay It Forward foundation has bracelets they use to emphasize the personal touch and a way to connect with another person live and in the moment at the time of the "act of kindness" is happening. If you don't want to invest in the bracelets, create a small card or token that you can physically pass along as a gesture and one that can be passed along to someone else. And a simple "thank you" is good enough.

Being present and in the moment opens you up to noticing more and more acts of kindness all around you and the opportunity to acknowledge what you see live and in the moment. This is part of your legacy in action while you are here on this earth, and it is a good feeling to know that you are helping to make the world a better place. I personally thank you for considering this as part of how you show up in the world.

Legacy is not what's left tomorrow when you are gone.
It's what you give, create, impact, and contribute today
while you're here that then happens to live on.
—Rasheed Ogunlaru, author

Conclusion

*We must be willing to get rid of the life we've planned,
so as to have the life that is waiting for us.*
—Joseph Campbell, American mythologist

Little did I know that I would be reliving so many situations and oftentimes deeply moving and emotional moments that mattered in my life. Many days I had the intention of writing and found myself so stuck that I could not write one word on paper. It was the opportunity to reflect on what was blocking me, and more so, what I really needed to release, let go, and reveal openly for others to see. I found this process to be extremely humbling especially when reflecting on how many real gifts have been granted to me as a result of my life's lessons, and the learning associated with them. Often when I was stuck, I was also in fear! Fear of being judged, fear of being ridiculed, fearing the imposter syndrome, my fear of failure, and most importantly for me, fear that finally my voice would be heard and no one would listen. I can share with you that fear is only an emotion that can be changed by our thoughts, feelings, beliefs, and actions. And that fear only becomes real if we let it go longer than ninety seconds! Yes, it takes less than 90 seconds to feel it, deal with it, and let it go because we control these feelings through our thoughts. Try it—it really works!

I could not even say the word "vulnerability" without it getting stuck in my throat; and let me tell you THIS has been the most revealing experience during this process. What I experienced, learned, and now embrace is that vulnerability is the gateway to more authenticity, love, integrity, and personal power, passion, purpose, and endless possibilities. Without facing it and embracing it,

CONCLUSION

I could not feel the peace and strength that I have more often than not. That said—the old limited beliefs working at the unconscious level still show up, and for me, this is the opportunity to choose what I want instead. I talked about the "tape recorder" in the book. Think about using your smart phone to record your thoughts, listen to them ... did you like what you heard? If not, rewind and start all over again until you get it just right. The same thing happens when these limited thoughts and beliefs show up. Listen, reflect, rewind, and record over them until they feel right for you! You have the power of choice!

On the days that I was able to write, it started with a thought or a conversation with a client or friend that ignited what I call a "download." I would begin to write, without much of an agenda, to find hours later some pretty good stuff that all tied back into how to **be seen, be heard, and be remembered**. The whole-brain thinking I unconsciously use as my decision-making process sometimes went from taking seconds to hours or even days to complete. The stories that showed up often were times in my life I had totally forgotten about—including the people that influenced me good, bad, or indifferent during those times. Many of these days of writing and pondering I found myself dealing with all kinds of emotions, and the process of moving through them was my way of continuing to discover, build, and bring my A-Game to the world. I was the reader of my own book! Everything comes from a place of helping to support my transformation and I hope it helps you along the way too.

Every single experience from the past and during this process was a reminder of how everything we do in life is by choice. Being present and in the moment allows us to *be* more than to *do* more. Our intuition is always there guiding us if we are present enough to recognize it and trust it enough to follow it. Awareness is the gift that keeps giving! Being curious about what we don't know is more than living from the past; it's fueling your future. When we are curious, we are interested in knowing something new about a situation or a person, making us interesting to others. Taking time to actively listen and engage with others touches the human spirit at its core level through the mere process of acknowledgment.

What I learned at a deeper level as part of this process was that it is not fair of me to always come from a place of giving without being open to receiving as well. I discovered that asking for what you want is a lot tougher when it's personal than when it's business related. The more I got comfortable with this notion, the more I shared it with my circle of influences as a discussion. And surprisingly, every single person said that finally they could do something for me! I was blown away by the generosity of others and also learned that this is the circle of influence and is a core part of the human spirit that we desire, deserve, and should embrace as well. Full transparency—this is still a work in progress and I suspect that it will be tested far more when this book is released.

That said; there are still people in the world that would rather sell, take, and operate from a scarcity mentality where money is their driving motivation. Now, there is nothing wrong with wanting to make money, but it is how we go about it that matters. Our core values drive our intentions, and for me personally it is more about abundance—that there is enough to go around—and if you value what you know and share what you value the money will come.

If you think of abundance as the glass is half full, this leaves a lot of room to fill it with what matters to you. Speaking of the glass is half full; there is some recent data on women at work that is worth adding here. There is a volume of media coverage for the books *Lean In* and the *Quest for Perfection* and others, as well as discussions of working women on what's wrong in their lives. Now there is a new generation of women leaders that are focusing on what is right.

Women are making personal choices between work and family—not the lack of advancement. Women leaving their jobs for independence are starting their own businesses, and according to the Global Entrepreneurship Monitor's 2012 women's report there are

CONCLUSION

126 million women starting or running a business. That represents more than one-third of global firms who now have women owners.

A new Accenture study, "The Next Generation of Working Women," found that 65% of women feel equal to men in the workplace and 66% see visible female role models. Many young women—like young men—put high-paying careers on the list of most important things in their lives. This is a new turning point for women who have put career success at the top of their list of values.

A study by Forbes Insights found that 24% of senior-level positions are filled by women. As of 2013 the leadership landscape is full of female role models who might have been in the minority, but they are no longer the exception according to the study. And here's the good news: the Center for American Progress projects that by 2030 women will hold 41% of senior posts. Most importantly, there is this force of women who are reshaping the future through the lens of confidence and optimism. Are you one of them?

I am excited about our future for women and for gender equality that supports men and women along their journey, and how to best evolve and grow in both work and life. We have come a long way, and it feels like we are accelerating the speed of change. I hope you jump on the opportunities you desire for your life.

The future is bright! The opportunities are plentiful! The power of choice is all yours! **What you think about comes about!** Think wisely and know that it's the moments that matter. Each moment creates the pathway for your life; know that you can change what isn't working through the power of thought, feelings, beliefs, and actions! It's your time to take action!

Let me close out this chapter by sharing a poem that has been speaking to me for most of my life:

DESIDERATA

Go placidly amid the noise and haste, and remember what peace there may be in silence. As far as possible, without surrender, be on good terms with all persons. Speak your truth quietly and clearly; and listen to others, even the dull and ignorant; they too have their story. ♦♦ Avoid loud and aggressive persons; they are vexations to the spirit. If you compare yourself with others, you may become vain and bitter; for always there will be greater and lesser persons than yourself. Enjoy your achievements as well as your plans. ♦♦ Keep interested in your career, however humble; it is a real possession in the changing fortunes of time. Exercise caution in your business affairs; for the world is full of trickery. But let this not blind you to what virtue there is; many persons strive for high ideals; and everywhere life is full of heroism. ♦♦ Be yourself. Especially, do not feign affection. Neither be critical about love; for in the face of all aridity and disenchantment it is as perennial as the grass. ♦♦ Take kindly the counsel of the years, gracefully surrendering the things of youth. Nurture strength of spirit to shield you in sudden misfortune. But do not distress yourself with imaginings. Many fears are born of fatigue and loneliness. Beyond a wholesome discipline, be gentle with yourself. ♦♦ You are a child of the universe, no less than the trees and the stars; you have a right to be here. And whether or not it is clear to you, no doubt the universe is unfolding as it should. ♦♦ Therefore be at peace with God, whatever you conceive Him to be, and whatever your labors and aspirations, in the noisy confusion of life keep peace in your soul. With all its sham, drudgery and broken dreams, it is still a beautiful world. Be careful. Strive to be happy.

—Poem written by Max Ehrmann in 1927

A-Game Terminology

A-Game: Building your authentic you! There is only one of you, and the world needs to know you. When you come from a place of authenticity, you are in your personal power (heard); living your professional presence and brand (seen); aligning with passion and purpose, collaboration, commitment, and contribution where you can make a difference and celebrating your gifts by paying it forward to others (remembered). This is a lifelong process of awareness (we don't know what we don't know until we know it), authenticity (self-discovery and development of the best you), alliance (build your circle of influence), affluence (commitment to an abundant life beyond money), and advocate (for others by paying it forward with your gifts). This continuum always starts with you!

Abundance: The opposite of scarcity that is an overflowing amount of wealth, resources, and the belief that there is more than enough for everyone. A shift towards abundance creates positive energy—and like attracts like.

Active Listening: Making a conscious choice and effort to hear and understand what others are saying. Creating this habit is the foundation for effective communication and helps you to use the reframe tool for clarity. Active listening helps you to understand, interpret, strengthen cooperation, and reduce conflicts and misunderstandings.

Adrenaline: A hormone produced by the adrenal glands during high stress or exciting situations that is part of the human body's stress response system. It is shown to increase strength to amazing degrees for a short period of time.

Affluence: Is when you have a great amount of something such as money, influence, or connections and the abundance of wealth and knowledge. Wealth is more than money; it is your wisdom, insight, knowledge, compassion, and intention of giving back to something greater than you.

Authentic: Being real, honest, genuine, original, trustworthy and true to one's own values, beliefs, and personality.

Authentic Leadership: Leading with your authentic voice (your truth), integrity, values, and ethics that identify your personal brand.

Awareness: Tuning into the concept that possibility is everywhere and it comes into view with awareness. **We don't know what we don't know until we know it,** and only then can we do something about it. **Awareness precedes action every time.** Awareness is one of the greatest gifts we have in life.

Blind Spots: We all have them. These are the biases that are buried in our unconscious mind that have been programmed by others' thoughts, feelings, actions, and what we have decided was important at the time. Because they are unconscious we don't know them as "blind spots" until we become aware of them, and only then can we decide differently.

Change: This is a stepping stone to something greater. Without change there is not opportunity to grow and expand and change what is not working for you. Embrace change as your best friend. It is going to happen anyway, so you might as well capitalize on it for your greatest benefit and outcome.

CLARITY: A process that helps you to get clear: **C**uriosity, **L**istening, **A**cknowledging, **R**eframing, **I**nspiring Action, **T**ransforming **Y**our New Story (what you tell yourself and others).

Collaboration: When one or more people decide to work together toward a common goal or purpose with passion and commitment.

Cortisol: The stress hormone that creates a lot of physical and emotional damage both short- and long-term. We can manage this by breathing into a situation with grace, ease, and love—raising our oxytocin levels that offset this stress hormone.

Common-Unity: When a collective group of people get together and rally around a common passion and or purpose that will help create change and action for desired outcome. It is easy to share insight, wisdom, knowledge, and appreciation when people are aligned with purpose.

Energy Leadership: Is a process that develops a style of leadership that positively influences and changes not only yourself but others. It is a one-of-a-kind attitudinal assessment based on an energy/action model that requires a certified provider to administer. It measures the level of energy based on your attitude, perception, and perspective of the world. The good news is we can alter our state by being aware and exercising conscious choice.

Entourage: These are deep meaningful relationships of reciprocity that differ from social and networking connections. An entourage is built on trusted relationships among those people you can call on and count on for support, resources, advice, and introductions for the long-term.

Emotional Intelligence: The ability to express, control, and own one's own emotions, along with the ability to understand, interpret, and respond to other's emotions. This includes self-insight and ability to manage your reactions to experiences.

Fears: Is that scared feeling that something is going to hurt you. We either go into fight, flight, or freeze that is a natural response to a real or perceived threat. It is pure emotion that can be shifted by our thoughts, feelings, beliefs, and actions to move from this place.

FOCUS: An acronym for **F**reedom to decide, **O**wning your own voice, **C**ommitting to connect with those that matter, **U**nifying your passion and purpose to create **S**uccessful strategies. P.S. If you are focusing on the why, you are focusing on the problem!

Fight/Flight/Freeze: These are the primary threat stressor responses. Fight and flight are activated when there is a chance you can outrun or outfight the attacker. Freeze keeps you locked in and activates a no-hope feeling. Fight and flight are innate and are an auto-response to help cope with danger. Freeze is like a deer in the headlights. Each of these stressors is temporary and can shift with your awareness, thoughts, beliefs, and actions to move forward in a positive way.

Gender Partnership: It's a movement that embraces both genders being responsive to assist each other in learning core competencies that can bring more balance in work and life. We have reached a turning-point in the labor force that makes this step a must if we are to contribute to a healthy economic environment.

Glass Ceiling: A set of attitudes, biases, and blind spots that prevent and oftentimes discriminate against women and minorities from advancement opportunities. These are usually unseen biases that create invisible (glass) barriers.

Glass Cliff: When you are asked to take on a high-risk opportunity that is ready to go over the cliff, and the company is willing to take on your leadership and what you can do. If it succeeds, you're in the club, if it fails, you are to blame and gone.

Glass Walls: An attempt to prevent someone from doing a different job or their own job effectively and/or moving to a position that has a room for advancement in the future. When working in a lateral role future opportunities are diminished as well. It often feels like we are blocked or restricted from growth and the ability to advance our career.

Imposter Syndrome: When one experiences self-doubt or feelings of inadequacy, even when the opposite is true and you just went for it: *I feel like a fake, I don't deserve xyz, I fear I'll be found out.* We have our internal dialog of self-doubt, self-worth, self-esteem, and self-confidence that overpowers reality at times. These are thoughts and feelings that can be shifted.

Influence: The capacity to have an effect on the character, development, or behavior of someone or something. It's the power to change an outcome and a compelling force that affects actions, behaviors, and opinions where it matters most.

Influence/Political Savvy: Understanding and utilizing the dynamics of power, organization, and decision making to achieve objectives, understanding how decisions are made, who the key decision makers are, who influences them, and increase visibility by active participation.

Mindfulness: Awareness or a state of active and open attention to the present. You are conscious of your thoughts, feelings, and actions without judgment—not good or bad; just different with a choice to change.

Mentor: An advocate for others. A resource, support, and help for peers and others that can learn from their experience. It is a critical resource in career development, giving support and guidance in a safe environment. Mentors help develop skill sets and ways to navigate the landscape of work and life. It's an investment to seek a mentor and to be a mentor to someone.

Networking/Making a Connection: This is a reframing of the word and of the feelings that come when people think about "networking." Typically it creates a stressed reaction and a dreaded experience, yet when it is reframed as "making a connection," the energy and mindset around it shifts in a positive and manageable way.

Neuro-Leadership: An institute led by David Rock focusing on the emerging field of study connecting neuroscience knowledge with the fields of leadership development, change management, and learning communities. It is a resource center for the latest developments on the brain.

Oxytocin: Known as the bonding hormone and the most powerful hormone that acts as a transmitter in the brain. It is greatly stimulated through hugs, kisses, and love, and is a crucial ingredient that makes us human. It reduces social fear, acts as a stress release, and increases generosity.

Reframe: Changing the way people see or hear things by finding an alternative way of expressing an idea, event, or situation. It shifts your mindset from a negative feeling or thought to a positive.

Scarcity: The concept of something being half-empty, not enough, or get-it-while-you-can because it won't be there if you need it. It is a fear that there is not enough for you that creates anxiety, uncertainty, and doubt.

SCARF: A brain-based model for collaborating with and influencing others. **S**tatus, **C**ertainty, **A**utonomy, **R**elatedness, and **F**airness. See www.neuroleadership.org for more details.

SHE-Change: A *sea change* is any widespread sweeping shift that affects all elements of a system. As Faith Popcorn indicates, in the coming decade we will see a *SHE change* in the way feminine power is incorporated in society.

SMART Goals: These are goals that are Specific, Measureable, Attainable, Realistic, and Time-sensitive. The more you work with this, the tighter and more effective you are at reaching and/or exceeding your goals in work and life.

Sponsor: Someone who is in an influential position to help you **be seen, be heard, and be remembered**—not by default, but with intention, attention, focus, and structure to help you navigate getting exposure and achieving advancement in your work and life.

Stretch Assignment: It's a project or task given to an employee that is beyond their current knowledge or skill level. It helps build, negotiate, and manage change, exert influence, and build alliances.

360-Degree Assessments: Feedback that comes from members of the employee's immediate work circle. Peer, supervisor, subordinates, and self-evaluation to help map and direct specific paths of development.

Unique Value Proposition: It's your brand and presence based on unique core values and differentiators. These intrinsic values are the "worth" of your brand—i.e. what you do and what it means to others. It is what sets you apart—your reputation, reliability, integrity, and results.

Universal Laws: As stated in *The Kabalion*, the universe exists by virtue of these laws and is the framework in which the world operates. They also have been known as "the keys" of all philosophies for thousands of years.

Law of Action: Everything in the universe moves, vibrates, and travels in circular patterns. The same principles of vibration in the physical world apply to thoughts, feelings, desires, and will, so that each thought has its own vibrational frequency unique unto itself.

Law of Correspondence: Tells us that the outer world is nothing more than a reflection of our inner world. It corresponds with your dominant patterns of thinking. "As within—so without."

Law of Cause and Effect: Nothing happens by chance outside the universal laws. Every action has a reaction or consequence and we reap what we sow.

Law of Compensation: Laws of cause and effect are applied to the abundance that is provided to us. The physical effects of our deeds are given as gifts, money, friendships, and blessings.

Law of Attraction: How we create the things, events, and people that come into our lives. Our thoughts, feelings, words, and actions produce energies that in turn attract like energies. Negative energy attracts negative, and positive energy attracts positive.

Law of Perpetual Transmutation of Energy: This is the most powerful, of all the Universal Laws, and it states all persons have within them the power to change the conditions of their lives. Higher vibrations consume and transfer lower vibrations. Keep your energy high and positive and watch miracles happen.

Law of Polarity: It's the law of mental vibration in which everything is on a continuum and has an opposite. We can suppress and transform undesirable thoughts by concentrating on the opposite pole.

Law of Gender: Governs all creation in its own gestation or incubation period for growth. It states in order for something to exist it must have unity with the opposite such as male/female, yin/yang, and positive/negative.

10,000 Hours Rule: The book *Outliers* by Malcolm Gladwell reviews research that demonstrates it takes roughly 10,000 hours of practice to achieve "mastery" in a field.

WAIT: Why **A**m **I T**alking? Is a process that helps you to participate in active listening that is far more effective than talking. By pausing and remembering to WAIT when you feel you are talking too much can help redirect to active listening.

Win/Win/Win: Is designed in a way that is mutually beneficial to all participants.

WINGS: An acronym to help you remember to spread your WINGS. Believe in your **W**orth; Trust your **I**nsights; **N**urture yourself; Have a big **G**oal; Devise a personal **S**trategy, and even the impossible dreams come true.

Whole-Brain Thinking: *Left-brain thinking* is the logical thinking about details while *right-brain thinking* is intuitive—thinking about potential and possibilities. *No-brain thinking* is the "freeze" mode of doing nothing and feeling stuck. *Whole-brain thinking* is looking at all sides in detail and connecting with your logic and intuition that moves you from being stuck to taking action.

For Research and Further Reading

Below is a list of research and whitepapers, books, and programs from some of the experts in the fields of leadership, gender issues, inclusion, women advancement, social intelligence, emotional intelligence, and the latest brain research.

Online Resources
Brain Reserve, Faith Popcorn www.faithpopcorn.com.
Braveheart Women www.braveheartwomen.com. Global Women's community.
Catalyst www.catalyst.org. Helps organizations and businesses build inclusive environments.
Center for Creative Leadership www.ccl.com. Leadership.
Center for Women in Business, Bentley University www.bentley.edu.
Cortisol.com. www.cortisol.com. Managing stress and weight gain.
The Disc Profiler www.thediscpersonalitytest.com. Assessment tools.
Harvard Business Review www.HBR.org. Resource website for business leaders and managers.
HeartMath Institute www.heartmath.org. Heart intelligence and stress management.
Hermann International www.hbdi.com. Brain research.
ION Advancing Women to Boardroom www.ionwomen.org. Board research.
McKinsey & Company www.mckinsey.com. Trusted advisor to world businesses and organizations.
Motivation Factor www.motivationfactor.com. Assessment tools for motivation and engagement.
Myers Briggs Foundation www.myersbriggs.org. Assessment tools.

NAWBO National Association of Women Business Owners www.NAWBO.org.
PEW Research Public Opinion Polling www.pewresearch.org. Attitudes and trends.
Small Business Administration www.SBA.org. Funding support for women.
TEDTalks *Ideas worth spreading* www.ted.com. High-impact live events recorded on every topic.
Women 2020 www.2020wob.com. Campaign for 20% of boards to include women by 2020.
A Women's Toolbox www.womenstoolbox.com. Online resource for entrepreneurs.

Print Resources

Gender Intelligence, Barbara Annis, www.baainc.com. Gender research and programs.
How Remarkable Women Lead, Joanna Barsh, www.mckinsey.com. Women's leadership.
Linked Out, Leslie Grossman, www.lesliegrossmanleadership.com. Entourage/Networking.
Good Girls Just Don't Get It, Dr. Lois Frankel, www.drloisfrankel.com. Women's leadership.
Take the Lead, Betsy Myers, www.betsymyers.com. Authentic Leadership.
Make Room for Her, Rebecca Shambaugh, www.shambaughleadership.com. Mentor/Sponsor.
She Negotiates, Victoria Pynchon and Lisa Gates, www.shenegotiates.com. Negotiations.
Never Eat Alone, Keith Ferrazzi, www.keithferrazzi.com. Networking.
Brag! The Art of Tooting Your Own Horn Without Blowing It, Peggy Klaus, www.peggyklaus.com. Self-promotion.
Lean In, Sheryl Sandberg, www.leanin.org. Advancement of women movement.
Why Men Never Remember and Women Never Forget, Dr. Marianne Legato. Gender differences.

Social Intelligence, Daniel Goleman, www.danielgoleman.com. Social and emotional intelligence.
Daring Greatly, Brené Brown, www.brenebrown.com. Vulnerability and fear.
Strengths Finder 2.0, Marcus Buckingham, www.strengthsfinder.com. Assessments tools.
Your Brain at Work, David Rock, www.neuroleadership.org. Brain research.
A Whole New Mind, Daniel Pink, www.danielpink.com. Author and expert on transformation and change.
Law of Attraction, Esther Hicks, www.abraham-hicks.com. Conscious creation.
The Keys to Living the Law of Attraction, Jack Canfield, www.jackcanfield.com. Conscious creation.
The Complete Vision Board Kit, John Assaraf, www.johnssaraf.com. Conscious creation.
The 5 Languages Series (relationships), Dr. Gary Chapman, www.garychapman.com. Relationships and tools.
Inspired and Unstoppable, Tama Kieves, www.tamakieves.com. Conscious creation.
Influence: The Psychology of Persuasion, Robert B, Cialdini. Influence.
The 7 Habits of Highly Successful People, Stephen Covey, www.stephencovey.com. Universal principles.

References

Accenture. 2013. "The Next Generation of Working Women." Accenture.com. Accessed November 1. http://www.accenture.com/SiteCollectionDocuments/PDF/The-Next-Generation-of-the-Working-Woman.pdf.

American Psychological Association. 2013. "Psychology Help Center." American Psychological Association. Accessed September 1. http://www.apa.org.

Barron, Lisa. 2003. "Men Negotiate Better." *Human Relations Journal* June 2003: 635-662.

Barsh, Joanna and Yee, Lareina. 2011. "Unlocking the Full Potential of Women in the U.S. Economy." McKinsey & Co. Accessed November 1, 2013. http://www.mckinsey.com/client_service/organization/latest_thinking/unlocking_the_full_potential.

Brown, Brené. 2013. "The Power of Vulnerability." TED Conferences, LLC. Accessed July 1. http://www.ted.com/talks/brene_brown_on_vulnerability.html.

Brown, Brené. 2012. *Daring Greatly: How the Courage to Be Vulnerable Transforms the Way We Live, Love, Parent, and Lead.* New York: Penguin Group.

Catalyst. 2012. "US Census Study." Catalyst. Accessed July 1. http://www.catalyst.org.

Cataylst. 2012. "US Women in Business Study." Catalyst. Accessed July 1. http://www.cataylst.org.

Cuddy, Amy. 2012. "Your Body Language Shapes Who You Are." TED Conferences, LLC. Accessed April 1. http://www.ted.com/talks/amy_cuddy_your_body_language_shapes_who_you_are.html.

Dorian, George, Miller, Arthur, and Cunningham, James. 1981. "There's a S.M.A.R.T. way to write management's goals and objectives." *Management Review* volume 70 (11): 35-36.

Gates, Lisa, and Pynchon, Victoria. 2013. "She Negotiates." Accessed May 1. http://www.shenegotiates.com.

Gladwell, Malcolm. 2008. *Outliers: The Story of Success.* New York: Little, Brown and Company.

Joint Economic Committee. Invest in Women, Invest in America: A Comprehensive Review of Women in the U.S. Economy. A Report by the Majority Staff of the Joint Economic Committee. (Washington, 2010), 7.

Kelley, Donna J., Brush, Candida G., Greene, Patricia C., and Litovsky, Yana 2013. "Global Entrepreneurship Monitor's 2012 women's report." Global Entreprenuership Monitor. Accessed November 1. http://www.gemconsortium.org/docs/2825/gem-2012-womens-report.

Kolb, Deborah. 2008. "Asking Pays off: Negotiate What You Need To Succeed." *Women Advocate.* Volume 13 (4): adaptation 1-2.

Lofton, LouAnn. 2011. *Warren Buffett Invests Like A Girl: And Why You Should Too.* Page 25. New York: HarperCollins Publishers.

Mehrabian, Albert. 1972. *Silent Messages: Implicit Communication of Emotions and Attitudes.* Belmont, CA: Wadsworth Publishing Company.

Popcorn, Faith. 2013. "2012 Predictions The SHE-Change." Accessed August 1. http://www.faithpopcorn.com/wp-content/uploads/2012/05/FPBR-Predictions-2012.pdf.

Rampell, Catherine. 2012. "Job Growth Isn't Just a Women's Issue." *The New York Times.* Accessed November1. http://economix.blogs.nytimes.com/2012/04/11/job-growth-isnt-just-a-womens-issue.

Rock, David. 2009. "Managing with the Brain in Mind." *strategy+business* (56): 2-10.

Small Business Administration. 2013. "Recovery Act and Small Business Jobs Act of 2010. Women Entrepreneurs Summit Series Report." Small Business Administration. Accessed August 1. http://www.sba.gov/about-offices-content/1/2895/resources/131371.

Thornton, Grant. 2013. "Women in Senior Management: Setting the Stage for Growth." *FORBES/Insights*. Forbes. Accessed November 1. http://www.forbes.com/forbesinsights/women_in_senior_management/index.html.

Vuong, Angeline. 2013. "Our Future Labor Force: Will Our Supply Meet Our Demand?" Center for American Progress. Accessed November 1. http://www.americanprogress.org/issues/immigration/news/2013/10/04/73645/our-future-labor-force-will-our-supply-meet-our-demand/.

About The Author

Carole Sacino is a visionary and respected thought leader, innovator, speaker, and a business and personal strategist. She has co-authored the best-selling, *Savvy Leadership Strategies for Women,* is the creator and host of the radio show, "The AWE Factor," and she is CEO of the thriving Turning Point Institute, which was founded in 2007. Ms. Sacino is a board-certified executive coach, certified in Emotional Intelligence, and is a Motivation Factor partner.

Ms. Sacino spent twenty-plus years in corporate America as a successful executive female leader with deep experience in sales, marketing, executive leadership roles, and running a business within a business.

Ms. Sacino stepped off the corporate success train leaving behind the title, suit, and paycheck to launch her business, the Turning Point Institute (www.turningpointinstitute.com), which designs, develops, and delivers solutions when the goal is to engage, commit, and motivate individuals and teams toward a common purpose or objective with results. She is known for helping others achieve clarity quickly with her natural curiosity, active listening, and affinity and inspired action for real transformation and change.

The book, *Build Your A-Game: Be Seen—Be Heard—Be Remembered,* is a natural extension to the work, passion, and commitment Carole has to help others to become the best of who they are in work and life. Carole has spent decades experiencing "adversity university" as a way to build awareness, authenticity, alliances, affluence, and advocacy for herself and others, and has a life-long commitment to pay it forward in the spirit of sharing what she personally knows and values.

Build Your A-Game
Be seen – Be heard – Be remembered

Author: **Carole Sacino**
Website: turningpointinstitute.com
Publisher: SDP Publishing

Available in print and ebook formats on:
Amazon
BarnesAndNoble.com
SDPPublishing.com

SDP Publishing

www.SDPPublishing.com
Contact us at: info@SDPPublishing.com

CPSIA information can be obtained
at www.ICGtesting.com
Printed in the USA
FFOW01n1745201114
8810FF